MANIFESTING
YOUR MAGIC IN THE 5D

Going Beyond the Laws of Attraction

JILL M. JACKSON

My heart is full as I think of everyone who helped me birth this book.

To my husband Daniel, thank you for working hard every day to allow me to realize my dreams. I look forward to the magic we will continue to create together. I love you more than I ever knew it was possible to love.

To my dad, Buddy, thank you for being my biggest cheerleader. No matter how often my journey has changed course, you are right by my side, offering any support you can. I am so blessed to have chosen a father who is also a mentor and friend. I love you so much.

To my beautiful mom, Gail, you were my greatest teacher of the Law of Polarity. I never knew the depths of deep grief until you stepped into the Other World. Learning how to live again taught me how to love even more. Thank you for being my Angel, my mom, and my friend.

To my sister Wendy, I'm so happy you walked this crazy road with me so long ago. Thank you for being my voice of reason when I needed it. We are beyond lucky that we can call each other sisters and friends. I love you more.

To my stepson Austin. Thank you for giving me the opportunity to be a mom. I am incredibly proud of the man you have become, and helping to raise you has been one of my greatest accomplishments. I love you, son.

To my editorial consultant, Gail Torr. I am forever grateful to the Universe for putting you in my path. You are an outstanding literary expert, and this book would not be what it is without your remarkable genius.

To Richard Crookes who designed the book cover, thank you. You hit a home run and took us straight to the winner's circle with this book. Your intuitive design skills are truly mind-blowing.

Thank you to all my spiritual teachers and mentors who guided me and graciously shared their knowledge with me.

And last but certainly not least, thank you to my Spirit Team, who always has my back. Thankfully, you have been able to retire the etheric two by four, as I have learned to listen to your guidance, even in the most subtle ways. I honor and appreciate each of you.

CONTENTS

INTRODUCTION

In a world sometimes characterized by chaos and confusion, countless people struggle with recurring setbacks, wrestling with persistent challenges while yearning for clarity and purpose. Within this landscape, as they faithfully attempt to apply the *laws of attraction* taught in the bestselling book *The Secret*, many find themselves disillusioned by the varied roadblocks encountered along the way.

Have you tried manifesting something specific and wondered what you were missing or lacking because it did not "happen" for you? You may have endured challenges and been saddened by the realization that you could not achieve success at manifesting the life of your dreams.

Throughout the past decade, there has been explosive growth and expansion in awareness and consciousness. Now is the perfect time to explore the perennial questions further: Why are we here, and what did we come here to accomplish? What are the tangible keys that unlock the mystical secrets woven into the fabric of our lives?

Manifesting Your Magic in the 5D: Going Beyond the Laws of Attraction aims to help you navigate the mysteries of the cosmos and reveal to you the timeless wisdom of the various spiritual laws of the universe. You will discover that there are fundamental principles that shape our reality, and when we learn the intricate dance of manifesting in the quantum fifth-dimensional field, we begin to unlock the potential to truly manifest our soul's desires without the previous disappointments while elevating our consciousness to a higher frequency.

I have become a powerful manifester, and the *Law of Attraction* and *The Secret* helped me along the way. I fell in love with the concepts and teachings in the books and the movie. However, after several heart-wrenching disappointments, I realized this recipe was missing some vital ingredients.

Following a period of grieving and mourning from my painful losses, I decided to go on a quest to find answers to why I failed to manifest the one thing I had always longed for. As I was guided to my answers, I realized that others were falling into the same trap of perceived "failure." As a psychic medium, many clients came to me seeking their own answers as to why they had not succeeded in manifesting their dreams— wishes they held on a deep soul level. Their pain, along with the wisdom I had acquired throughout my journey, compelled me to write this book. I became committed to sharing my personal experiences.

In Chapter One, you will see how I stumbled and fell in a significant area of my life in which I could not manifest what I wanted more than anything. I fell into the depths of depression, not only from my inability to achieve what I wanted so badly but also from feeling defeated in a type of "manifestation failure" that made me feel even worse.

Chapter 2 encourages you to ponder the additional Spiritual Laws, inviting contemplation about these other jewels that work in conjunction with The Law of Attraction. In addition, I offer insights from my background and experiences in helping guide others to navigate their lives through the illuminating compass of Universal truths.

In Chapter 3, we explore a summary of the book *The Secret*, along with the principles of the law of attraction. Humanity has evolved enough to understand a deeper level of awareness. To illustrate this, I introduce a fictional character who feels disappointed by the law of attraction. However, upon reflection, she recognizes the influence of other factors, such as soul contracts, which alter her initial manifestation request into something more extraordinary.

Chapter 4 introduces ten additional Spiritual Laws that support the law of attraction, demonstrating how they are connected to assist us on our journey through life. Within these pages, I delve into the myriads of these Universal Laws that harmonize and complement each other. The beauty of the Spiritual Laws is that they can be interwoven to create a beautiful tapestry of direction and personal empowerment.

Chapter 5 delves into the etheric realms of past lives, karma, and soul contracts, unraveling their intricate roles in the manifestation process. These esoteric concepts play a pivotal part in our journey towards materializing our desires, shaping the path we travel and the outcomes we encounter along the way.

Before embarking on the manifestation journey, we must grasp the essence of our soul path and purpose. Chapter 6 examines the pre-incarnation agreements we make regarding our life blueprint, which comprises both soul challenges and soul opportunities. Understanding who we are, and our inherent destinies creates more profound manifestations and fulfillment.

In Chapter 7, we uncover the captivating realm of frequency and vibration. Quantum physics reveals all beings are connected. It is imperative to transition our consciousness to the quantum field to enhance our ability to manifest. This chapter outlines seven transformative shifts you will experience when you raise your vibrational frequency.

In Chapter 8, we embark on a journey into the philosophical concept of unity, unraveling the intricate web of interconnectedness that binds us all —a concept known as quantum entanglement. We embrace the delicate balance between using the law of attraction for personal gain and extending our manifestation energy to benefit humanity. I coined the phrase L.I.F.E. —Limitless Information for Everyone. As we learn to tap into universal intelligence and align our vibrations with the frequency of the divine or Source, we transcend the emotions of greed, lack, and fear in our consciousness.

In the last chapter, you will be guided on creating your masterpiece—an extraordinary life that reflects your most profound dreams and desires. Chapter 9 presents a comprehensive roadmap comprising nine essential steps aimed at assisting you in manifesting the highest version of yourself. Each step is designed to empower you, providing practical tools and insights to navigate the complexities of life with clarity and purpose.

As I often enjoy doing things in other areas of my life, I decided to step outside the proverbial box in terms of the composition of this book. I have included a fictional story based on real-life situations to complement the book's nonfictional concepts. The story's beginning unveils itself in the Prologue, and the ending is revealed in the Epilogue. I sincerely hope you enjoy these fictive bookends, which use real-life examples to underscore the concepts explained in the book further.

In closing, I encourage you to explore the companion workbook explicitly designed for this book. At the end of each chapter, I offer journal prompts and suggestions for you to write about how the ideas pertain to areas and situations in your own life. After all, my goal in disclosing the grief from painful chapters of my life is to help others with similar challenges, not only to transcend them but to transmute the seeming negative into something positive and powerful.

One of the greatest lessons of this wild and extraordinary human experience is learning to honor our grief and transmute setbacks and failures into something even more profound. Through deep revelations and understandings, we are provided with beautiful gifts to evolve. I pray that this book is one of those gifts for you.

If you enjoyed my book, *Secrets of the Secret*, you'll love this revised edition, packed with additional new material.

Infinite Blessings!
Jill M Jackson

PROLOGUE

The alarm clock blasted its deafening buzz way too early as far as Mandy was concerned. One of her New Year's resolutions was to stop hitting the snooze button multiple times, so she forced herself out of bed to face the day. The strong aroma of French roast coffee brewing helped ease some of her disappointment that it was only Thursday. As Mandy enjoyed her coffee, she reflected on the exciting seminar she had attended the weekend before. The speaker's words echoed in her mind as she replayed the message. The speaker was a Law of Attraction expert, and her promise to everyone in attendance was that they could manifest anything their hearts desired.

Still charged with adrenaline from the energy of the weekend, Mandy had come to the bold conclusion that she would take charge of her life and begin manifesting all her dreams. As she walked to the other room to grab her journal, she congratulated herself on getting out of bed without hitting the snooze button, giving herself more time to reflect on all the things she would manifest using the Law of Attraction. Her cat Theodore followed, loudly meowing that it was time for his breakfast. "Give me a moment, Teddy. I'm going for my journal while my inspiration is still bubbling!"

Mandy made a mental note to take her journal to work with her so she could write down some dreams while she was eating her salad at lunch. "The first thing I will write," she confided to the seemingly disinterested feline, "is how John's proposal will unfold. I'm sure it will happen on Valentine's Day next month!" Licking his paws after a delicious breakfast, Teddy reflected on his own dream. *I wish Mom would go ahead and schedule that appointment with the animal communicator. That way, I can relay the message that I despise John. Why can't Mom see he is selfish and self-centered and can barely tolerate that I'm still here with her? I, her faithful companion! The nerve of him! Surely there is a kind-hearted man out there who will shower her with love and give me the proper ear rubs that I deserve!*

As Mandy bundled up, preparing to face the brutally cold Michigan morning, she gave Theodore a big hug and kiss goodbye. "Make yourself useful today while I'm at work," she joked. As she drove to work, she ruminated on how she would manifest a job promotion. After all, she deserved this promotion. She had been with the company for five years, was never late, and always kept a cheerful outlook. *No, this is not my dream job*, Mandy admitted to herself, *but it pays well, and I get two weeks' vacation every year.*

Since Sunday, Mandy had been printing her name with the title supervisor after it. The speaker at the Law of Attraction seminar taught that if you write things down, the energy becomes stronger, and it is more likely that you will manifest what you desire.

As Mandy walked through the office plaza where she spent most of her waking hours, she felt slightly frustrated as Rebecca stopped her at the coffee station to gossip about the new cute guy in accounting. Mandy was far more interested in organizing her desk, excited to celebrate the promotion that she knew was coming any day now. Plus, Mandy thought to herself, *I'm committed to John, and I'm looking forward to marrying him and starting a family.* Her doubts, along with her sister's warnings about John, tried to force themselves into the corridors of her mind, but Mandy was quick to dismiss those negative thoughts. She loved John and knew he would eventually come around to enjoy the things that made her heart soar. Her wish list was to rescue animals and spend time on sunny sandy beaches. However, John was a workaholic who never was available to take her to Florida beaches, despite her asking him countless times. *Maybe I can hopefully manifest a beach trip for us, Mandy thought.* Smiling politely at Rebecca, she grabbed her coffee and headed to her desk. As she settled in to begin her monotonous duties, the phone at her desk rang. Tim, the human resources manager, was on the line and asked her to see him. Mandy almost skipped to his office as she knew her promotion was about to be offered. *Wow, this Law of Attraction stuff works quickly!* she exclaimed.

"Good morning, Tim," Mandy chirped as she sat in the chair by his desk. "I hope you enjoyed your vacation." Tim nodded nervously, moving quickly on to this discussion. "Mandy, you have been with our company for five years now, and we truly appreciate your service and loyalty to our firm." Mandy took a deep breath, anticipating the excitement of the job promotion announcement she was about to receive. Tim paused. "However, our shareholders approved a larger year-end bonus than normal for the President and Chairman, so we are forced to make some adjustments to accommodate the budget. I'm terribly sorry, but we will be eliminating your position," Mandy shook her head in disbelief. This was not possible. "I don't understand," she said. "What am I supposed to do?" She continued, "Is there any severance or compensation for my years of service?" Tim smiled proudly as he explained to her that he had secured two weeks' severance for her. Feeling as if she might pass out at any moment, Mandy blurted, "Two weeks? Are you kidding me? After five years of loyal service and never missing any days besides my vacation? This is what my loyalty and hard work is worth to this firm?" Eager to end the unpleasant exchange so he could devour his donut waiting patiently behind him, Tim pushed the paper toward Mandy for her to sign.

Mandy fought back her tears as she cleaned out the desk that had been home to her for so many seemingly never-ending days over the years. As she drove home, allowing the sadness to envelop her in waves of sobbing and despair, Mandy screamed to no one in particular, "Why was I not able to manifest this promotion? I did everything instructed at the workshop!" Thankfully, she would at least have the faithful Teddy awaiting her return. Petting his velvety orange and gray hair always calmed her down.

Immediately upon walking into the house, Mandy put down her boxed desk materials and called John In her message, she told him she really needed to talk to him. Washing the streaked makeup from her face, she decided to wait until Monday to start looking for another job. Maybe John would end up pro-posing early, she mused. This thought brought a smile to her tear-stained face. Manifestation revisions would have to start right away! She would stay calm, prepare a cup of Earl Grey tea, and work on her Law of Attraction journal to manifest the proposal. For good measure, she decided to go ahead and visualize the gorgeous home they would live in together. For a moment, the voice in her head reminded her that she and John had vastly different visions of their dream home. John wanted a condominium near his city office, whereas Mandy preferred a single-family home with a large yard for all the animals she planned to rescue and let play. *I am sure if I visualize strongly enough, John will come around to see how special a house with a*

large yard will be. Mandy began cutting out houses and pho-
tos of wedding gowns from the countless magazines she had
collected.

As she looked out at the bleak midwinter day, Mandy
wondered what she had done wrong in manifesting her job
promotion. *She vowed that she would need to put more effort into
the other things she wanted to manifest.* She also allowed herself to
dream of sunny days at the beach and felt a fresh wave of disappointment that John did not enjoy the beach. She shook her
head, wondering how on earth she was still living in Michigan
when there was no one she knew who disliked the snow and
cold as much as she. *Oh, well, at least with my new tools from the
seminar, I'll be able to make trips after I'm married to John,* Mandy
reassured herself.

After enjoying the last sip of her tea, Mandy decided to go
look for the business card of that psychic her friend Denise
had told her about. Denise had raved about the psychic's accuracy and life-changing revelations. Maybe it was time to try
her. When she had mentioned it to John in the past he had
laughed, telling her not to waste her time and money on such
nonsense. Thinking about this reminded her that John had
not called her back. She told herself he was probably stuck in
meetings and would call later. They had an upcoming date for
Friday evening, but Mandy decided she would tell him about
her job loss on the phone. As if on cue, Teddy jumped up on
the desk and landed on the psychic's card. A clear sign! She
would dial the number. What harm could it possibly do? Miss
Thelma answered the phone on the third ring and told Mandy
that fate must have intervened, as she had a cancellation that
afternoon. "Can you be here at 3:00?" Miss Thelma asked.
Nervously, Mandy told her she would be there.

As Mandy pulled into the small house's driveway, she was
not sure what to expect. What she found on the other side of the
door when Ms. Thelma opened it was the farthest thing from

what she had imagined. Ms. Thelma was short and old. As her bony fingers reached out to shake Mandy's hand, Mandy felt a chill run down her back. What could that sensation be all about? Never had she been in someone's presence who made her feel so very calm yet energetic at the same time. This sensation was foreign and confusing to Mandy, yet she dutifully followed Ms. Thelma into her reading room. Mandy looked around the room in childlike delight. There were shiny crystals everywhere. When she was a small child, Mandy had a special affinity for rocks and crystals. The pleasant scent of sandalwood and frankincense curled and danced through the air from Ms. Thelma's dragon-shaped incense burner. Ms. Thelma introduced Mandy to the gorgeous black cat sitting at her feet. "This is Magic, my protector," Ms. Thelma explained. "We have traveled together through many incarnations." Mandy was not sure she believed in reincarnation but decided to remain open. She quickly concluded that she would not share this experience with John, as she knew he would disapprove of her choice to visit this old woman.

Mandy's attention eventually returned to Ms. Thelma herself. She noted the wise and kind hazel eyes looking back at her. She had never experienced such intense eyes. But before she could ask Ms. Thelma about her job and career opportunities, Ms. Thelma declared to her that she was not in the right relationship. "He's not for you," Ms. Thelma whispered, "and he's been unfaithful." Mandy immediately stood up, prepared to leave. "You must have me confused with another client," she demurred. "My John would never cheat on me!" Mandy suspected Ms. Thelma's gaze could pierce right through her head, but the old sage smiled compassionately at her. "You and John have been in a karmic relationship from your past life," Ms. Thelma bluntly revealed. "The relationship was brought back to teach you about The Law of Polarity while balancing the karma from your past life together in Greece."

Still reeling from the shock of what this eccentric old woman told her, Mandy recalled John speaking of wanting to visit Greece. *How would this woman know this?* Mandy asked herself, attempting to shake off the words she had just heard. Ms. Thelma continued, "Your world is turning upside down to help you land on the proper path of your soul purpose. The animals are waiting for you to rescue them and find them proper homes. Your soulmate will be at your side as you walk this new path because the two of you agreed to this soul contract before this incarnation. And by the way, you will be leaving Michigan, never to return."

Rattled and confused, Mandy paid the woman and headed for the door. Before she could close the door behind her, the wise woman counseled, "Always pay attention to the signs and synchronicities of the Universe. Release your control, my sweet child, and surrender, and the riches of the Universe will fall at your feet."

As Mandy turned on the ignition, she silently cursed Denise. *How could Denise refer me to this?* Unable to calm herself, Mandy drove a block up the street, out of Thelma's field of vision (she hoped), then pulled over to call Denise. "She told me John was cheating on me, Denise! She must have me confused with someone else." Denise assured her that 95% of what Ms. Thelma had revealed to her had happened. As Mandy replayed the outcomes prophesied by Ms. Thelma repeatedly in her mind, she had a strange feeling in the pit of her stomach. She decided to have an early dinner, try to forget about the past hour, and go to bed early. When she woke up Friday morning, she realized that John had never called her back. There was a text from him saying he was working late and would see her the following night. Excited about their date that night, Mandy reminded herself to practice the Law of Attraction all day.

However, her excitement was short-lived, as later that night, across the table at the Italian restaurant they loved so much, John was breaking up with her. "How can you do this?" Mandy cried. "We've spent four years together, and I thought we would get married!" John, fidgeting, looked into his glass of chardonnay and declared he had fallen in love with the new account manager his firm had hired three months ago. "Mandy, I've never felt like this before, and we want the same things out of life. We are going to be moving in together next month. I'm sorry to tell you this in public, but I thought it would be best for both of us."

Mandy cried herself to sleep that night, feeling like her world had completely crumbled around her. Aggravating the excruciating disappointments of the past few days was a sense of inadequacy that she had failed miserably at the Law of Attraction. As she woke up on Saturday morning, however, she felt a little stronger. She decided she would give the Law of Attraction another try. Using the knowledge she had gained at the seminar, she would manifest her long-desired move to Florida. Posthaste, Mandy told her friends and family that she would be moving to Florida to begin her new life. Yet, after several weeks of job-hunting in Florida and no prospects, Mandy began to lose hope. Why were her manifesting techniques not working? As she stared at the flames dancing in her fireplace, the burning embers seemed to remind her of her failures.

A few days later, Denise called Mandy and invited her to dinner, saying she had some exciting news to share. Depressed and deflated, Mandy decided to go, hoping it would make her feel better. What Denise told her over dinner sent Mandy into a tailspin. "Our company has a job opening in Mobile, Alabama, and you are perfect!" Denise exclaimed. "Alabama? Are you joking? Why on earth would I want to move to Alabama?" Denise reminded Mandy that her job search in Florida had turned up zilch. "Why don't you go back to see Ms. Thelma?"

Denise said excitedly. "After all, everything she told you was accurate!"

Mandy scheduled an appointment with the gifted old sage as soon as she could get in. Ms. Thelma immediately assured Mandy that the move to Alabama was a key puzzle piece in the divine plan she had put in place with her Spirit Guides before being born. Ms. Thelma taught her about some more Spiritual Laws that must be honored along with the Law of Attraction. "You have successfully applied the Law of Action by moving forward on your desire to move to Florida. You researched the area. You called around and put in resumes. Now, you must bring in two other Spiritual Laws to assist you. The Law of Relativity instructs you to move forward on this relocation to Alabama, choosing to view it positively. Begin to speak about the new job and the move in an optimistic, powerful way. This energy will begin to shift your vibrational frequency in transformative ways." Seeing that Mandy followed her, she continued, "The Law of Faith must be put into place. This is a time to let go of the control that you think you have and surrender, trusting that the Universe has your back. Love awaits you, and surprises are in store for you, but only if you have faith."

As Mandy drove out of Michigan, leaving behind the only life she had ever known to move to a state she had never been to, she felt like she was jumping off a cliff into a river of murky uncertainty. Gazing over at her faithful sleeping cat, Mandy boldly proclaimed, "I am on a mission to discover why I could not manifest my dreams and desires when I did everything we were taught at the Law of Attraction seminar. I admit I feel lonely and afraid, but Ms. Thelma's soothing words play a melody of hope in my heart."

And with those words, she headed south to Alabama.

CHAPTER 1

MY SECRET STORY

I'm positive each person reading this book has had both success and "perceived" failure by using the techniques outlined in *The Secret*, the best-selling book by Rhonda Byrne. While I enjoyed the book and feel that it helped raise the level of awareness and consciousness at the time of publication, I also believe it is time for humanity to explore the deeper spiritual laws surrounding the concept shared in *The Secret* and why, sometimes, the outcome looks different from what you were trying to manifest initially. In other words, the basic concepts within the Law of Attraction and what was written in *The Secret* are valid spiritual laws. However, I have come to recognize that it is time for us to explore the deeper meanings of these ideas.

One of my personal "perceived" failures prompted me to write this book. Later, I will discuss why I use the term "perceived failure." It is sometimes difficult to share such raw emotions and losses with others, yet it is imperative to discuss these life events so that others may be helped along their journey. When we hear or read about another person's experience that mirrors our own, there is an opening for feeling understood. This creates more opportunities for healing and growth. So please join me as I share my private personal journey with each of you.

Many years after my special wedding day to my now ex-husband, I asked him to list some things about me that made him fall in love. His response: "Oh, that is an easy one. Your positive attitude and belief that you can attain any goal you set your mind to!" Of course, being a smart husband, he listed many more attributes! But this story is based on that one character trait I have always been proud of. During my life, I have always been able to accomplish and manifest anything I set out to do. Except in one area.

My ex-husband and I married on New Year's Eve in 2000 on a beach in Southern California. Not only was I joining a life with him, but I was also instantly a stepmom to an adorable 5-year-old named Austin. Up until this experience of being a stepmother to Austin, I was unsure of whether I wanted biological children. Austin, who was the best kid anyone could hope for, provided a quick answer to that one for me. I was 36 years old, and suddenly, the proverbial biological clock was heard ticking loud and clear.

As I have always done before embarking on my next life journey, I began my positive affirmations and visualizations. I set my intention to have a healthy baby and become a biological mother. *The Secret* had not been published then, but I was familiar with the concept of manifestation, as it had always worked for me. Before this time in my life, I had been able to manifest anything I set my mind to. My friends and family always shook their heads in disbelief about what I successfully manifested for my life!

I knew how the process of manifesting worked. The key to proper manifesting is to think about and discuss your desire as if it had already happened. I "saw" our little girl! The smile on her face was radiant! In November 2002, my positive visualization worked, as I found out I was pregnant! I had never felt that kind of elation in my entire life! My ex-husband and I had created a baby! I shared this news with everyone I could tell and immediately began searching for a tall building I could stand on and shout my news to the world!

Unfortunately, the screaming that followed four weeks later was the sound of wailing. At six weeks pregnant, I lost our baby. Desolation crept in, followed by a period of deep sadness and grieving.

After the initial shock wore off, I told myself that many women miscarry the first time. I remembered how important positive visualizations are to any want, wish, need, or desire. OK, maybe I did not visualize enough or in the right way. This time, I decided to name our little girl. She would be called Jackson after the town of my birth. I began addressing her by name when I talked to her as if she were already a family member. In September of 2003, Jackson was conceived! I thanked God and the angels for bringing us such a special gift. One of the most beautiful experiences a woman may have is the gift of carrying a child in her womb and feeling that connection right away. It is a feeling that is difficult to describe, but most women immediately develop a special relationship with the child growing inside them. There are flashes of daydreaming where you can live an entire lifetime in mere moments. And trust me, I had many such moments as I contemplated how amazing and different my life would be once baby Jackson was born. However, my daydreams and joy were cut short as a meager four weeks later, at six weeks pregnant, the miscarriage pains began again. Devastation does not even start to describe the feeling of loss. For many of us women, there is a shame attached to not being able to bear children. Feelings of inadequacy began to creep into the corners of my soul.

After another period of grieving, I remembered how I have never given up and always been able to achieve anything with the right belief system and positive affirmations. I just "knew" pregnancy number 3 was on its way!

This time, my meditations grew longer and deeper. The special time that Jackson and I shared gave me so much hope. I even bought her a beautiful ballerina pillow that would be her first gift from me, her momma. I prayed and prayed. My family prayed and prayed. Our prayers were answered in April of 2004! But once again, six weeks into the pregnancy, our little girl was gone again. As those of you know who have been through these tragedies of lost pregnancies, your world is shaken to the core. Some women become angry at God. You may ask, "Why me? Why do other women bear multiple children, and I can't even have one? Where is the justice in women who continue to get pregnant—often when they do not even want their babies—while I keep losing mine? Am I not good enough to be a biological mother?" Intellectually, I knew this was not the case, as I had become the best stepmother I could be to then 9-year-old Austin. And Austin wanted a baby sister. I felt such sadness and hopelessness that I was unable to give him a sibling.

Still, after a while, I declared, *OK, time to get back up, dust myself off, and make sure that my positive visions, affirmations, dreams, and desires coincide with my true reality.* I created a vision board. I started reading more self-help books about attracting anything you want into your life by using the correct techniques given by each author. I meditated. I prayed. I ate healthy food. I consulted with the best, most innovative fertility specialists. My ex-husband and I spent thousands of dollars on special blood tests to make sure there was nothing physically wrong. I endured countless procedures, many of them extremely painful, to make sure all my female organs were working properly. I repeated the mantra, "Ask, and it is given," repeatedly every day. Defeat was not a word in my vocabulary.

I theorized that I was given these challenges so that the appreciation would be infinite when I held our baby Jackson for the first time. Come August of 2004, great news arrived once again! "Wow, this positive affirmation stuff really works!" I marveled. I thanked God for this miracle. I promised Him that I would be the best mother on the planet. But then, at six weeks pregnant, you guessed it: pregnancy number 4 had ended. "Why is this happening to me, God? What have I done to deserve this? I have always been an honest, ethical, spiritually solid, good person. It's not fair!" I screamed. It seemed the tears would never stop flowing.

During those three years, I had suffered severe endometriosis. After each loss, I had to go through surgery to remove the relentlessly binding spider webs of tissue. It was like cancer in that once it started growing, its tentacles would reach out in search of the next organ to wrap around as if trying to cut off the life force for good. My gynecologist had informed me that a fourth surgery would have to be the last one since the scar tissue, along with the endometriosis, was causing me never-ending excruciating pain. He recommended IVF as our last hope. This was a lot for my ex-husband and me to take in. There was also a huge cost factor involved in this decision. Being 38 at the time was going to decrease the likelihood of success. None of the doctors and specialists could find a reason for my miscarriages. I had the eggs of a 20-year-old I was told, as if this would paint some silver lining to my picture. My ex-husband and I agreed to go forward on one condition. This would be our last attempt at becoming parents together. Due to the daily pain, which was interfering with my quality of life, the next step was a hysterectomy. All right, time for the big guns of The Law of Attraction, positive affirmations, positive visualizations, another vision board, and, for good measure, acupuncture was added to the mix! This was my time to be a mother! No holds barred! No fear, no worries, no negative thinking.

The day of the egg retrieval, it was music to my ears when our doctor grinned and told us that he had retrieved more than enough perfect eggs. Three days later, on a gorgeous Southern California day, it was time for the embryos to be implanted. Five had made it and were graded the highest quality of A+. We decided to implant three since this was our final chance of bringing home the gift of a bouncing baby girl. Our acupuncturist was by my side not only with the perfect number of needles placed for greater success but also keeping me in an ideal state of calm, positive affirmation, and bliss. I just knew God would not let me down this time, as He knew this was to be my last chance for motherhood. I now understand that God does not decide our fate or whether we have a baby or do not have a baby. But at the time, I had that belief system.

During the three days of bed rest that followed, I had never prayed so much. I visualized our baby Jackson attaching to my uterus and holding on for dear life. "Hold on tight, baby girl," I told her. We talked about all the things we would do together as we entered the next chapter of our lives while guiding baby Jackson on the first chapter of hers. I laughed, I cried from joy, and I made sure I appreciated and enjoyed every moment of being a new mom. I thanked God and Jackson for choosing me to be her mom. I knew with all my heart that she was growing inside me. And she was, as I found out three days later! "You're pregnant, Jill! The IVF worked perfectly for you!" I knew I could do it. I knew I would be successful at practicing positive affirmations and visualizing what I wanted more than anything. I knew this Law of Attraction concept had given me a fresh renewal on life! I could not wait to tell others about this amazing technique! Imagine how many people this would help to achieve anything their hearts desired!

As fate would have it, I was again given only four weeks to embrace motherhood, as I lost baby Jackson at six weeks. A part of me died that day. I lost all faith. I lost my will to survive. And I lost all my female organs several weeks later as they rolled me into surgery for my total hysterectomy.

This was my "secret" story.

After my hysterectomy, it took about a year or two before I could walk into a store and witness a mother with a new baby and not run from the store sobbing. I recall the day when my sister Wendy and her husband David came to visit me with news shortly after my hysterectomy. As I sat down, the looks on their faces said it all. I knew they were pregnant. I cried, both from happiness at their wonderful news and sorrow as my losses sank deeper into the darkness of my soul.

When it was getting closer to the time for my sister to give birth to their son, family, and friends started asking me if I was sure I still wanted to be in the delivery room. Honestly, I had to give deep thought to this question. On the one hand, my grief was as fresh as the morning dew, as it had only been a few months since my dream of biological motherhood was stripped away. On the other hand, I had been there for the delivery of my sister's two other children, Payton, and Reagan, and I did not want to miss out on the beautiful miracle of her and her husband's son, Tyler, entering the world. I'm so grateful I chose love over sorrow in deciding to be a part of baby Tyler's birth. However, the gut-wrenching pain was still so fresh that I was not even able to stay for Tyler's first birthday party, which took place close to a year after my hysterectomy. As everyone started singing "Happy Birthday," all I could think about was my baby girl and the fact that I never had the chance to celebrate her being born, much less rejoice over each birthday celebration. As the singing grew louder, I felt my throat constricting and genuinely felt as if I were suffocating. I ran from the party before I caused a scene or did anything to hurt my family's joy.

I have often pondered whether the grief is stronger for a woman who is not able to conceive at all or for the woman who conceives, feels the elation of impending motherhood, then loses her baby. I guess in the grand scheme of things, it does not matter which grief is greater. Both scenarios are losses that will alter the lives of the women forever.

There were days when my sorrow was so bad it was hard to get through the day. I read books on grief and loss and finally decided to find a grief counselor to work with. On our first visit, my ex-husband and I shared our very personal story of joyous expectation, then loss, in the hope that the counselor could somehow ease our pain. After hearing about all my lost pregnancies, the counselor said, "I know exactly how you feel. I lost three pregnancies myself, but luckily, I was finally able to have a child." My sobbing grew louder. My ex-husband said some choice words to her, and we left. I could not believe someone could be so heartless when their very job was to comfort the grief-stricken. I never attempted grief counseling for my lost pregnancies again. I am sure there are many excellent, caring grief counselors out there who have helped women heal from their losses; it just did not turn out that way for me.

To make matters worse, my ex-husband and I were in a very tumultuous custody battle over Austin. Austin's biological mother had found out about my miscarriages. She claimed that God knew I was an awful stepmother and, therefore, He was not allowing me to bring a biological child into the world. Her new husband's favorite word for me was "barren bitch." She repeatedly told the court and the judges that I was not a mother and, therefore, my parenting ability should not factor into the court's ruling. I will never forget the day I found out she was pregnant again with a bouncing baby girl. I wondered how I could survive in such a cruel universe where the woman who mocked my inability to carry a child to full term could be blessed with another child, and a girl, at that. After all, I had treated Austin as if he were my biological child. My ex-husband and I were finally granted full custody of Austin, who started calling me Mom when he was around 12 years old. Even though my marriage to Austin's father did not last, Austin and I remain close, and he still calls me Mom. One day, when Austin came home from school, he said, "Mom, it occurred to me today that God knew you needed a child, so that's why you ended up being a mother to me." My eyes still well up with tears when I think about that sentiment from Austin. And he had no idea that day how very deep his wisdom was. I *had* become a mom. Just because you did not give birth to a child does not mean you cannot be a great parent to a child. Or perhaps your parenting comes in the form of animal fostering and adoption. Or maybe you are an amazing teacher who provides parental support to children who may not have very much of it at home. There are myriad ways to offer mothering other than giving birth.

After much soul-searching, I decided I did not want to live the rest of my life harboring these destructive emotions of anger and sorrow. Before coming to this conclusion, however, it took years of inner personal work and struggle to shed the resentment, shame, humiliation, and utter sadness that had become part of my daily life. Sometimes it felt as if for every two steps forward, I had taken three steps backward. But I have always been positive, so I did not give up.

For those of you enduring your inner demons, possibly resulting from a loss such as mine, I encourage you not to give up on your efforts to work through the pain. It is possible! Reading books about other women's losses and experiences and how they got through them helped me so much. Journaling also helped a great deal. For some people, grief counseling has done wonders. Finding a group to be a part of has proven useful for others.

Yet even after releasing the negative emotions that had become so entrenched in me, I still did not have answers as to why I was not able to manifest a child when I had been successful at every other thing I had ever put my mind to. So, I went on a quest to find the answers I sought. My search led me to various psychics, mediums, past-life regression training, and many meditations. Our journeys are often rugged and winding, yet I can promise each of you reading this book that if you stay the course on your path, the answers will always appear. And for me, as I traveled this road, new jewels of wisdom were provided to me at each fork along the way.

The rest of this book will share my insights on what I found and the truth that resonates deeply with me. I began using Jackson as my last name professionally in honor of my little girl who did not make it into physical form but who lives in my heart forever.

The next chapter of my journey begins here.

INVITATION TO EXPLORE

This is a perfect place to stop reading for now and give thought to areas in your life where you have tried to manifest something and have not been successful. Write about your experience and how it made you feel. Did you feel anger, shame, resentment? Did you lose your belief system? What, if anything, have you done to help heal your pain? Simply putting words to paper can be quite powerful in helping us first to see exactly what emotions we are experiencing and then to help us decide what the next steps are for working through the loss.

CHAPTER 2

BEYOND THE LAW OF ATTRACTION: UNVEILING THE SOUL'S BLUEPRINT

After reading my personal story, you may suspect I do not believe in manifestation or the Law of Attraction. This is certainly not the case, as I have spent my entire life manifesting many things, including becoming a published author. For example, years ago, when I decided I wanted to write and be published, I started telling people I was a writer even though the only things I had written were client engagement letters for my CPA clients. Hardly a romantic edge to the launch of a literary career! Whenever a stranger and I struck up a conversation and asked about my profession, I would tell them I was a writer instead of mentioning my current profession.

I knew how to use the technique within the Law of Attraction by speaking of what you desire in the present tense as if it were already so. Within a year or two, I was finally published in a newspaper in Ojai, California. Trust me, though, much had to go into manifesting this, including studying, reading books on writing, taking writing workshops, and, well, just writing. This conformed to the Spiritual Law called the Law of Action, but I will go into that concept more deeply in a later chapter.

This book is about going deeper beyond *The Law of Attraction*. It is about learning to tie the concepts together, with awareness of soul contracts, past lives, and Spiritual Laws. I have discovered the deeper reasons why not all Law of Attraction techniques work for us all the time.

The Law of Attraction is only ONE of the Spiritual Laws of the Universe! When I discovered that there are many more Spiritual Laws we can learn and apply, I felt like a kid in a candy store. I wanted to sample all of them! When I discovered how great and interconnected they are, I wanted to share this knowledge with others.

I have also learned that until we truly know ourselves, we cannot understand what we want to manifest. Take some time to think back over your life. Would the things you choose to manifest now look the same as the things you wanted to manifest five, ten, or even twenty years ago? Probably not. Why is this? As we go through our lives, we have experiences, we learn lessons, and we have opportunities for soul growth. Our awareness increases along with our awakening as we ponder thoughts such as: "Why am I here?" and "What did I come here to accomplish?" Hopefully, through this process, we will grow and begin to awaken to different and diverse concepts.

Another example of how I used the ideas in *The Law of Attraction* is when I realized I would no longer stay on the course as a CPA and money manager. I felt satisfied that I had accomplished everything I set out to do in that career and I knew it was time to jump off the cliff and trust that my parachute would open. I began telling people I was a psychic medium. I came out of the proverbial psychic closet even before I started reading for people professionally!

Before we go any further, let me introduce myself. I am a natural-born psychic medium. For those of you who are not exactly sure what this means, allow me to give you a crash course in the work of a psychic or a medium. A psychic perceives information from someone regarding the past, present, and future. A gifted psychic can also communicate with your Spirit Guides. A psychic can guide you in areas such as love, career, and even life purpose. A medium receives information directly from loved ones who have crossed over to the other side. A genuinely talented and ethical medium will be able to provide evidence such as names, dates, descriptions, and specifics of how your loved one passed over. I have the gift of psychic and medium, which is both a privilege and a huge responsibility, depending on the day. I go deeper into my journey of being born a psychic medium in my debut book, *Mississippi Medium*.

I am honored to be a member of Best American Psychics, founded by Shay Parker. Shay was initially a bit skeptical until she started having paranormal experiences. While she was searching for someone to help her and provide answers for her, she found that there were no directories of psychics and mediums, at least none who had been repeatedly blind tested. This eventually led to the creation of her company, Best American Psychics. Shay created a directory in which every member was double-blind tested, with ethics and integrity also required of the members. In 2012, I was accepted into the group, won the Social Activism Award for my work with animal rights in 2014, and then, in both 2015 and 2016, was awarded the prestigious Psychic of the Year Award.

Even though I was born with the gifts of intuition, prophecy, and mediumship, I did not share this fact with many people. On the one hand, I wanted to live a normal life, study hard, play hard, and have lots of friends. On the other hand, I honestly believed everyone could see Spirits. I have always been book-smart, graduating a year early from high school. It was not until years later that I realized most people around me did not "know" what I knew. It took me a long time to learn to listen to my intuition, though! One of my Spirit Guides insists that I needed a metaphorical two by four to the head before I finally started paying attention! Ouch!

We are all born with degrees of intuition. Some have it stronger than others, yet everyone can learn to tap into and strengthen their intuition. It serves us in many ways to increase our intuition. One of the great joys of my life path is being a spiritual teacher to others! I revel in the delight of watching my students become either professional psychics or mediums themselves or simply use their intuitive abilities to help guide themselves along their chosen life path.

Now I want to revert to the part about trying to live a normal life! I went to college and became a CPA (Certified Public Accountant). I lived and worked in Southern California, where I was a money/business manager for the entertainment industry. An entire book could be written about my amusing experiences in that profession, but I will save that for another time!

After accepting that my dream of becoming a biological mother would not happen, my lupus symptoms started coming back full force. I had initially been diagnosed with lupus in my twenties, yet I was able to get the disease into full remission. Looking back, I realized that our Spirit Team will get our attention in ways we may not see at the time, to gently remind us of what we came here to accomplish. The stress from running a fast-paced and successful CPA firm eventually caused my illness to return. I ended up in a hospital and came close to death. The stress affected me differently from my fellow CPAs because this was not the life path I had chosen before incarnating. I had already broken the stereotype of old-bald-male-accountant, so why the hell couldn't I make an about-face, give my weary left brain a rest, and start relying on my right brain? You would have enjoyed being a fly on the wall the day I called my dad and explained that the college degree he had paid for was wonderful, but I had decided to sell my CPA firm and become a professional psychic medium! Thankfully, I chose parents who were both incredibly supportive of my choices, whether to pass the difficult CPA exam and open my firm or jump ship and start talking to Spirits every day. And yes, we do choose our parents before each incarnation. We'll explore this exciting concept in the chapter on Soul Contracts.

In meditation, I have seen that each of us has a group of Spirit Guides to help us navigate through life. I refer to mine simply as my Spirit Team. And even though I was a successful CPA and money manager, I quickly realized this was not my soul purpose. After much meditation, contemplation, and input from other psychics, my decision to sell my CPA firm came easily. It was time for me to take the leap of faith, give up a comfortable six-figure income, and step back onto my true path using the gifts with which I was born. It was during this time that I took various spiritual classes and became a Reiki Master, an energy healer. I encourage everyone to find a reputable energy-healing teacher to study with. Everything is energy, and the more we learn to work with that energy, the easier our lives become. I also took tarot classes and learned to use the tarot as a divination tool to enrich my psychic readings. Each class, workshop, book, and seminar propelled me further along my journey and assisted me in finding the life path I had "signed up for," so to speak.

However, I still did not have all the answers I needed and wanted regarding why the tools offered by the Laws of Attraction had not worked for me in becoming a biological mother. Just as a delicious soup requires all the key ingredients to be edible, manifesting only works when you use all the essential elements, not just one.

After exploring various healing modalities and spiritual growth movements, participating in group sessions with other psychics, engaging in "conversations" with my Spirit Guides, and becoming certified in past-life regression, I finally understood why the instructions and suggestions in The Law of Attraction books may not always work. It is time to broaden our perspective on what The Law of Attraction does for us personally and to embrace a new awareness that manifesting is not about greed or merely our personal desires. I am excited to share some of the other spiritual laws with my readers, which will foster a deeper understanding. In later chapters, we will explore how these Spiritual Laws interact and how they necessitate a synergistic union with our past karma and soul contracts.

Before we incarnate in each lifetime, we consult with our Spirit Guides, and they assist us in designing our soul's blueprint. The blueprint is a dynamic plan and roadmap, capable of adaptation based on free will and the choices made during one's lifetime. Its primary purpose is to aid in our spiritual development, helping us navigate our earthly journey with purpose and clarity. Just as architects can revise their plans, humans can use their Spiritual Law of Free Will to amend their blueprints along the way. In chapter 5, we delve deeper into this intriguing subject.

All that matters is the here and now, this moment. The Law of Attraction, suggests we think, speak about, and vividly imagine the situations and things we want to manifest. You can see that this is taking our awareness to some future timeline and bringing it back to the present moment. It is one of our life challenges to master the concept of leaving the past behind while keeping our feet firmly planted in the present. It does not serve us to live in the future, to go through life with the mantra of "what if" and "as soon as." Yet, I believe the Law of Attraction principles about how to speak your wants, wishes, and desires in the present tense is much more powerful than telling them in the future tense. Let me give you an example here. Instead of saying, "I want my soul mate—whom I will meet soon—to be loving and kind and respectful of me," a much more powerful statement would be, "My soul mate is loving, kind, and treats me with respect. Thank you, Universe, for this gift!" This brings the realization of your desires into the now, into the present moment, and creates an energy surge that helps bring this into reality. In the chapter on The Spiritual Laws, we will discover how to blend the Law of Attraction with the other Spiritual Laws. We will also explore how our past lives influence our current lifetime and how important it is not only to get to know ourselves but to fall in love with ourselves (before being able to manifest certain things).

Another concept to ponder is this: Faith is another Universal Spiritual Law. There are no accidents or coincidences. We all have an opportunity for soul growth: learning to trust and surrender. We invite our thoughts and words into existence via the Law of Attraction. Also, if we genuinely believe the Universe will provide everything we need when we need it, there is unending beauty in trusting and surrendering to this absolute truth. This quote from Albert Einstein shows such truth and splendor: "There are only two ways to live your life. One is as though nothing is a miracle. The other is as though everything is a miracle."

Humans seek knowledge. The type of knowledge and the depth of that knowledge will more than likely fluctuate over time. Gaining knowledge is like rowing a boat down a beautiful stream. You may have a deep desire to row your boat for a while, yet something stirs within you, telling you to pull the boat over to the shore and rest. The experience you had rowing that boat will stay with you forever. Perhaps you learned new rowing skills, or you experienced an aspect of nature you had never witnessed in the past. If you increase your knowledge and awareness over time, nothing is lost. This is how these concepts work for us. And then come the synchronicities that follow. When our awareness increases, we are naturally and suddenly drawn to subject areas and concepts that would never have interested us in the past or would not have been understood for lack of awareness. As we set out on a spiritual quest or path, new doors suddenly swing open. We meet new people who generously share their wisdom and experience with us. We learn to take what resonates with us and kindly leave the rest behind. This process is much like a caterpillar blossoming into a beautiful butterfly. And everyone's spiritual path and awakening looks different, with various timelines unfolding uniquely. The goal is to not judge ourselves or others as we awaken. And even though most of us will probably not realize enlightenment in this lifetime, there is joy and excitement in uncovering universal secrets and truths.

Let us take a moment to think about the word *truth*. Among Merriam-Webster's definitions of truth are: "the body of real things, events, and facts: actuality (2): the state of being the case: fact (3) often capitalized: a transcendent fundamental or spiritual reality b: a judgment, proposition, or idea that is true or accepted as true." Can you now see why your truth may differ from someone else's? And how your truth may even change over time as you evolve? When we take time to ponder this one word and concept and identify how our truth has evolved over the years, we can more easily have compassion and understanding for those who may not share our truth. There is amazing power and an opportunity to raise our vibrations when we practice nonjudgment and compassion, not only toward others but ourselves as well.

Have any of you wondered why *The Secret* was not published until 2006? Why did this book become one of the best-selling spiritual books ever when its principal concept was covered and discussed as early as the 17th century? It all has to do with divine timing and the level of awareness of the people incarnated on the planet. Remember that everything is about frequency, a fundamental that we will look at in greater depth in the chapters on The Law of Attraction and The Spiritual Laws. Frequency is a signal which indicates eagerness and readiness. Teaching and raising awareness must have been part of Rhonda Byrne's soul contract or blueprint. Her Spirit Team would have gently nudged her toward writing the book. Just as mine has alerted me, we as a species are ready to explore the next levels of the concepts covered in this book. In so doing, we find the proper balance between manifesting only for ourselves, in an energy of personal aggrandizement and manifesting for all sentient beings. After all, we are all connected!

The next era of manifestation for our wealth, happiness, health, and loving relationships will gradually begin to extend to ALL of humanity! It is not simply about the "I" but about the "We." It is about the greatest of manifestations for Unity and eventually, Divine Consciousness!

Later chapters will also offer ways to discover your personal life path and describe how like-minded souls will begin to gather and form local communities and online groups that support one another on a selfless level of love, understanding, sharing, and growth. These groups are affectionately known as our Soul Tribes. My online Soul Tribe, the High Vibe Tribe, is a community that truly makes my heart sing.

I am hopeful that each of you who reads the remainder of this book will experience aha moments, moments of deep inner knowing. Remembering our authentic selves and the soul groups we were in before this incarnation helps guide us to the ultimate fulfillment of our karmic missions. As time will reveal, when we strive to manifest good things for all of Creator's children, our Mother Earth will begin to vibrate at a level of energy not witnessed in a long time.

Many of you are already familiar with some of these concepts. However, for others, much of this material will be new.

Wherever you may be in your awareness, knowledge, and beliefs, I ask that you read the remainder of the book with an open mind. What I have found both on my journey and in my professional life as a psychic medium reading for my clients is that sometimes things we are exposed to may not resonate at the time the material is introduced, yet when our psyche is ready to grasp the true meaning, cellular memory will bring the concept back into our awareness. We can experience those moments of understanding. Awareness is like a window to the soul. The deeper the awareness, the easier for us to peek through the window. There is much wisdom in the ancients waiting for those who seek. Ever-increasing awareness of our human rights and potential. Open your arms wide and welcome the treasures that await you. You will be forever grateful for what you accomplished along the way.

INVITATION TO EXPLORE

I invite you to grab a cup of hot tea and journal about any aha moments you have had along your path in life. Whether you feel you are on the correct soul path or are about to face the proverbial fork in the road, write whatever comes to mind and heart. Journal about things you desire to manifest for everyone. Examples may be world peace and the end of wars, the end of hunger, and one of my passions, the end of animal abuse and suffering.

CHAPTER 3

POWER OF POSITIVE THINKING

What is the Law of Attraction? The Law of Attraction is one of many Universal Laws. In simple terms, this spiritual law teaches that like attracts like, and what you focus your energy on, you will attract to you. This makes perfect sense, as everything is energy, and quantum physics has proven that thoughts and intentions do have the power to create our reality. The essence of the law is that if you think positive thoughts, you will attract positive experiences, and conversely if you think negative thoughts, more negative experiences will show up in your life.

The Law of Attraction has been recognized for eons of time. In 1877, the term" law of attraction" appeared in print for the first time in a book written by the Russian occultist Helena Blavatsky. Since then, this concept has been put forth by many New Age and New Thought authors, from Louise Hay and Esther and Jerry Hicks to Rhonda Byrne, when her best-selling book *The Secret* was published in 2006.

Why have Law of Attraction books been so successful? It is because we are souls inhabiting human bodies. Our human selves come with egos, personalities, and numerous physical desires. We crave achievements, relationships, and shared experiences. Many of us have been conditioned to believe that our main objectives in life are to fall in love, marry, have children, enjoy fulfilling careers, and accumulate wealth for luxury homes and fancy cars. But is this really the true purpose of our human experience? In my view and experience, the answer is a resounding no! However, that does not mean we cannot achieve the things we think we desire.

But there is one caveat: It must align with our soul's contract.

In simple terms, the book *The Secret* teaches that our thoughts create our reality. Ms. Byrne explains that our emotions, attached to the desired outcome, play the leading role in achieving said outcome. She even advises people to speak about their wishes and desires as if the outcome has already happened. I agree that if we are going to practice manifestation, we should think, speak, write, and *feel* our desires as if they are already in our physical reality. At the same time, we must always remember that if, for some reason, our desired outcome does not come to fruition, there are much deeper and sometimes complicated reasons for this "perceived failure."

As previously mentioned, I prefer using the term *perceived failure.* Let me explain what I mean by this. Just because we are presently unable to manifest something we *think* and *believe* we want does not mean we have failed! In fact, when we look back and reflect on things in our lives that did not manifest, we can usually come to an understanding of why they were not to be.

For example, I have come to realize that my true joy comes from being a mom to animals that I fondly refer to as my fur babies! As an added blessing to my true joy, I had the wonderful opportunity to experience motherhood through helping to raise my stepson, Austin.

So, looking back and going through the discovery process of my soul blueprint, I have been able to reach a level of understanding, acceptance, and even approval for the experiences that have shaped my life.

Matthew 7:7 says, "Ask, and it will be given to you; seek, and you will find; knock, and it will be opened to you." The Buddha said, "All that we are is the result of what we have thought. The mind is everything. What we think, we become." Jesus and Buddha were referring to the foundation of the spiritual law, the Law of Attraction. The provocative question, however, is the much deeper dynamic of why this law sometimes does not work or may not work within the desired time period. Have you ever listened to the lyrics of Garth Brook's song "Unanswered Prayers?" Here are a few lines from this beautiful song: "Sometimes I thank God for unanswered prayers. Remember when you're talkin' to the man upstairs? Just because he doesn't answer it doesn't mean he doesn't care. Some of God's greatest gifts are unanswered. Some of God's greatest gifts are all too often unanswered...Some of God's greatest gifts are unanswered prayers."

That is fine, but the question remains: Why would God (or Source) *not* answer our prayers, and how could the positive energy of focused thoughts, feelings, and intentions sometimes fail to bring our desires into being? This is where it can get quite complicated, but it is something that we should be talking and teaching about so that others do not feel the dejection and depression I did when I was unable to manifest my little girl. The grief from my loss was deep enough without adding the emotion of what I describe as "manifestation failure" to the mix. It is my passion to explore the possible reasons that something you are trying to manifest does not come to fruition as you had hoped.

This is where the concepts of fate, destiny, free will, and soul contracts enter, and how they relate to The Law of Attraction.

First, let us define these words. According to Merriam-Webster, fate means "the will or principle or determining cause by which things in general are believed to come to be as they are, or events to happen as they do." Per Dictionary.com, destiny means the predetermined, usually inevitable, or irresistible course of events." From my perspective and understanding, I believe in the general concept of fate and destiny as it pertains to our blueprint. And to add more flavor to the soup, we must also throw in soul contracts!

Soul contracts are established between our souls and our Spirit Guides before each incarnation. As we learned in Chapter 2, the soul contract is a blueprint that acts as a guide or map for our life choices. I also believe in the philosophy of free will, which holds that humans are free to make choices not predetermined by prior causes or divine decree. Life experiences do not fit into nice, tidy packages with a pretty bow on top. Events are not always absolute. Within this reality, our consciousness grows, diving deep into the interactions between destiny and free will. If destiny and fate predetermine events to give us opportunities for soul growth, yet we have free will to take detours along the way, can you see how complex things may become when you add the Law of Attraction to the mix?

Have you ever wondered why some people seem to lead charmed lives, yet others have many challenges? Some old souls have reincarnated many times, and young souls have not experienced many lifetimes. Younger souls have easier life experiences, and by the same token, older souls have chosen more difficult incidents to delve into during their lives. We can joke with our Spirit Team and exclaim, "What the heck was I thinking when I agreed to this?" Yet, it is important to recognize that our Spirit Team loves us unconditionally and would never have agreed to life experiences we were not equipped and prepared to manage. However, it is understandable that, at times, we may benefit by having a heart-to-heart with our

Guides and asking for extra assistance during challenging times.

Why is it that *The Secret* sold over 20 million copies and was translated into 50 languages? Because so many of us were obsessed with the idea that we could think of ourselves as rich, thin, and healthy, *no matter what*. The book claims that if we think angry thoughts, we will manifest events and circumstances that will in turn cause us more anger. I would like to ponder the situations and events in which someone is the innocent victim of a senseless crime. Based on the principles outlined in *The Secret*, this person must have thought angry thoughts of violence and therefore brought on this crime themselves. I do not share this belief. There are times when karma may be strongly involved in an event. If someone is raped, does this mean the victim had thoughts of violence or hostility and somehow brought this brutality into their lives? Of course not. This spiritual law is complex and is not as simple as: "Think positive thoughts, and you will thereafter be rich and successful and able to afford any house or car your heart desires."

Are the Flint, Michigan residents responsible for the toxic water they are living with? If you interpret the principles outlined in *The Secret* literally, an assumption could be made that every person in Flint harbored thoughts of illness and toxicity. The true cause of Flint's water situation is the city officials' poor choice to bring the water from the Flint River rather than from Lake Huron, where it had always come from. How on earth could anyone claim that every single resident of Flint created their nightmare of sickeningly dirty water? This concept does not make sense, no matter how much you think about it. But let us ponder this a little more. What if some of Flint's victims had somehow caused toxicity, whether physical or emotional, to others by their actions in a past life and had chosen of their own free will to live in Flint and experience the consequences of the poor choices that led to the traumatic events? Perhaps

41

we can expand this concept by asking, "Is it possible that some of these residents have an even higher purpose than balancing their karma?" Maybe they chose a life path of service that would bring awareness to this injustice and then crusade to help fight the city and get clean water to their fellow residents. As you can see, the possibilities are endless.

Staunch proponents of the Law of Attraction argue that negative thoughts and emotions can even put you in a path or scenario like natural disasters or terrorist attacks. It has been noted that this teaching mode can unwittingly instill fear in people or, even worse, have them blame themselves when some unfortunate event strikes their life. At one time in Southern California, I suffered a massive fire in my neighborhood. I had to wake up in the middle of the night, gather my stepson and my animals and a few personal belongings, and drive away from my home not knowing if it would be there when I got back. I do not believe I had harbored thoughts and feelings of a calamity, thus bringing this frightening experience into my reality. This does not resonate as truth for me. Perhaps Mother Earth needed cleansing in the area where my neighborhood was located. I do not know why some things happen to some people and not to others. No one does. But I know that there is unfathomable depth and intelligence to everything that happens, which warrants our contemplation and, ultimately, our reverence.

What rings true for me in the Law of Attraction is that we have been given the unbelievable gift of creating our realities. We are powerful creators and, collectively, the masters of our universe. Studies have shown that we use only a small portion of our brain's capacity. When they want to manifest something in their lives, I tell my clients that the Law of Attraction works in stages. You first have a thought about something you want to manifest. Next, write down what you would like to manifest using the present tense. Begin to think about and imagine how this will make you feel. Feelings are keys to success.

Within the Law of Attraction is a vortex of possibilities. Just as an automobile has many parts that must work together before you can drive, your wants, wishes, and desires also have complex and intricate moving parts that must converge in perfect divine synchrony.

I will use an example of the Law of Attraction in action and an entertaining twist. Let's meet Carol. Carol desires a change of scene and thinks about manifesting a move to a new city. In a flash, the white sandy beaches of South Florida come into her awareness as she remembers seeing Miami Beach in a movie. This thought comes in and feels exciting to Carol, and since Carol has studied and read all about the Law of Attraction, she knows she must write down her desire to move to Miami Beach. Carol then starts thinking about the types of friends she may meet when she arrives. She even starts researching the demographics of neighborhoods and condominiums. Carol finds online forums about community groups and the general energy of the area. Next, she begins to plan a visit to Miami Beach. Can you see how all of this builds the energy? These are all positive and exciting thoughts, combining the Law of Action and the Law of Attraction. (We will discuss this concept in greater depth in a later chapter.) Suppose that after Carol has continued with these positive thoughts and plans, even vacationing in Miami, she returns home and gets a job transfer to a *different* city. Does this mean Carol was not successfully practicing the Law of Attraction, and that manifestation did not work for her? Not at all! Something *much better* happened to sweet Carol! Carol's soul mate/beloved/life partner awaited her in that different city! By practicing the Law of Attraction, Carol intensified the energy behind the desire for change! And this mobilization of energy nudged her in an unexpected direction, yet it all ended very positively. How about another plot twist thrown in for good measure? Once Carol met her life partner in the city, she did not think she wanted to go to, she discovered that her life partner had also dreamed of moving to Miami! And all of this had stemmed from her initial thoughts of manifesting a change!

I would also like to share a personal story about how the Law of Attraction worked for me. I journaled (in the present tense) about my true love and life partner five months before I met my husband, Daniel. My description filled two pages with what I wanted, wished for, and desired in my mate, and Daniel possesses them all. Daniel and I have often asked ourselves why we did not meet earlier. We lived in the same small city for four years, went to the same places, and even knew some of the same people, yet we did not meet until years later. We both had done enough individual spiritual work to understand that we were not ready for each other before we met. We still had personal soul growth and exploration before we were ready to merge our lives. I thanked the Universe for Daniel before I met him, and I still thank the Universe daily!

I am deeply grateful for the pioneers of the Law of Attraction teachings, whose vision and dedication have shaped our understanding of how our thoughts and beliefs influence our lives. These trailblazers have illuminated the profound connection between our mindset and our experiences. Their work has empowered countless individuals to harness the power of positive thinking and intentionality to transform their lives. By sharing their insights and experiences, they have created a legacy of hope and possibility, encouraging us all to embrace our potential and manifest our dreams. Their contributions have been invaluable in spreading the message that we have the power to shape our reality through our thoughts and intentions. This established a solid foundation for manifesting, but a structure requires more than just a sturdy base.

We surely could not leave our discussion of the Law of Attraction without including Esther and Jerry Hicks! Esther Hicks channels a group of spiritual teachers who call themselves Abraham. According to Esther, Abraham's teachings affirm our fundamental well-being and help us recognize and nurture joy's power in achieving all that we desire in life. Abraham has described themselves as "a group consciousness from the nonphysical dimension." They have also said, "We are that which you are. You are the leading edge of what we are. We are that which is at the heart of all religions." If you have not been exposed to these inspiring teachings, I highly recommend reading books, attending a workshop, or listening to the audio recordings of the channeled sessions. The Hickses have been remarkably generous in offering a wealth of YouTube clips from their workshops. The love, wisdom, and power that Esther Hicks has channeled from this group is phenomenal.

There is absolute truth in the teaching that everything in our Universe is based on energy and vibrational frequency and that positive thoughts, intentions, and beliefs do raise your vibrational frequency. I hope and pray that sharing my knowledge, beliefs, and experiences with others will lead to a deeper understanding of the spiritual laws underlying the Law of Attraction.

When most people are asked why they want to manifest something, whether it is a new house, relationship, or anything, the answer is invariably, "this new thing will make me happy." Do you agree that finding happiness is the true meaning of life? Is it the goal? What does happiness mean to you? Do material things really make us happy? I believe that to know happiness, it must first reside within us. If someone purchases their dream car yet does not possess inner happiness, the euphoria from buying the car will quickly fade, and the person will find themselves searching for the next item to buy or the next accolade to receive as they attempt to fill an inner void. There is obviously nothing wrong with enjoying material pleasures. However, if we do not feel happy with who we are and practice gratitude for our lives, the material objects will mean much less to us.

Strive to find your true north of happiness. Joy, gratitude, and a genuine love of life are the main qualities to greet each day with.

I want to end this chapter with a powerful quote from Gandhi. As you read and digest what he says here, pay attention to the importance of the meaning behind his words regarding our authenticity and destiny: "Keep your thoughts positive, because your thoughts become your words. Keep your words positive because your words become your behaviors. Keep your behavior positive because your behaviors become your habits. Keep your habits positive because your habits become your values. Keep your values positive because your values become your destiny."

INVITATION TO EXPLORE

Now is your opportunity to journal with a more personal, ego-driven goal in mind! Sit down and journal all your hopes, dreams, and desires. Remember to write them down in the present tense. I can assure you that this works if your desires are in harmony with other aspects of your life and life path. Feel the emotions you will experience once the manifestation is anchored into your current reality!

CHAPTER 4

UNLOCKING THE SECRETS OF THE UNIVERSE: AN INTRODUCTION TO SPIRITUAL LAWS

Our universe consists of Laws or Principles meant to govern our lives. Many people differ on how many Universal Laws there are and what they consist of, so for my book, I will be discussing the ten Spiritual Laws that resonate as truth for me, in addition to aligning to and supporting the Law of Attraction.

UNIVERSAL LAW #1—LAW OF ATTRACTION

This is the Universal Law most people are familiar with. It says your thoughts create your reality. Like attracts like. Using this law constructively, the focus is on positive visualizations, expectations, and manifesting your dreams and desires.

There are many tools that can assist in mastering the Law of Attraction, including vision boards, journaling, visualizations, and mantras. However, as I will discuss throughout this book, this is only one of the Spiritual Laws, and to truly master this law, a deep understanding of subjects such as unity, collective consciousness, and soul contracts is crucial as the true basis of the very core of this law is to bring truth and balance to manifesting in a context of spiritual expansion.

Since I devoted an entire chapter to the Law of Attraction, I would like to spend more time discussing some other Spiritual Laws and how they are interwoven.

The main key in mastering this law is to know ourselves on a deep spiritual soul level. With knowledge comes awareness. With awareness comes understanding. And with understanding, the clarion call to our true destiny can be heard.

UNIVERSAL LAW #2—THE LAW OF VIBRATION

According to quantum physics, everything comprises energy, including humans, animals, plants, trees, rocks, water, and even inanimate objects such as furniture. Everything has a vibrational frequency. Thoughts, words, and sound carry a vibration. As humans, we can set our vibrational frequency either up or down. Just because we cannot see vibrations of objects with our physical eyes, does not mean that animals, plants, and inanimate objects do not carry an energetic frequency. Research conducted over the years by Dr. Masaru Emoto proved that the molecular structure of water responds to stimuli such as music, and even to the thoughts and intentions of human consciousness. His bestselling book *The Hidden Messages in Water* details these experiments. Dr. Emoto proved that when positive words were spoken to a glass of water, the water, when frozen, formed beautiful crystals; conversely, when negative words were spoken, ugly crystals formed.

The Law of Vibration is the pillar and foundation of the Law of Attraction. Before we can attract something to us, a frequency or pattern must be created. Imagine cosmic waves of energy culminating in and around what you wish to manifest.

To master this Universal Law, we must remember that our thoughts, emotions, and words carry a vibrational frequency, not only within our physical bodies but, in turn, throughout the entire universe. Positive words, emotions, thoughts, and actions raise the vibrational frequency of everyone on the planet, including Mother Earth.

We can learn a great deal from this fictional character Maya. Maya, an aspiring artist, has been struggling to find inspiration for her next big painting. She has been feeling frustrated and disheartened, doubting her abilities, and fearing that her creative spark has faded. One day, while reading Manifesting Your Magic in the D5, Maya learns that her thoughts and feelings emit vibrations that can attract experiences and opportunities into her life.

Maya decides to put the principles of the Law of Vibration into practice. Each morning, she takes a few moments to meditate, focusing on the feelings of joy, excitement, and passion she experiences when she envisions herself as a successful artist.

As Maya's thoughts and emotions shift to a more positive and confident state, she starts to notice changes in her environment. She receives an invitation to exhibit her work at a local gallery, meets a mentor who offers valuable advice, and finds herself inspired by the new energy around her.

By aligning her vibrations with her desired outcome, Maya experiences a surge in creativity and motivation. Her next painting becomes one of her most successful pieces, and she feels a renewed sense of purpose in her artistic journey.

Through her practice of the Law of Vibration, Maya discovers how her positive energy can attract and manifest the success she had been longing for.

Try to practice this Spiritual Law in your everyday life. Give great thought to how energy works. Strive to make your contribution to the vibration of our planet a positive one. Create some uplifting mantras that you will think about daily or say aloud. Choose your words carefully. Wake up each day and speak at least a few words of gratitude. Focus on bringing alignment and harmony into a positive vibrational frequency in all aspects of your life and begin to witness the magic unfold!

Universal Law #3—The Law of Action

This Spiritual Law shows us that proactive action is required to bring our dreams, wishes, and desires to fruition. When we act toward a goal, we generate a movement or force of energy that activates the Law of Vibration and, consequently, the Law of Attraction.

Let us examine a few examples of the Law of Action in motion. If someone desires a new car, some ways to signal the Law of Action are to begin researching the type of car you want or taking the car for a test drive.

If you desire to understand meditation or spiritual practice, action is required to generate the energy around this. By thinking about grasping the foundations of a deep meditation practice, the Law of Vibration begins to create a code or frequency around this subject. To attract this type of spiritual practice into our lives through the Law of Attraction, steps of actually doing something to acquire this knowledge would be required. We could drive to the bookstore to discover the perfect book to help us get started. Perhaps we are introduced to a spiritual teacher specializing in the type of meditation we want to practice.

If the desired outcome is for a mate or partner to share our lives with, the chances of this person randomly knocking on our door are remote—even if we have practiced the positive intentions of the Law of Attraction. The Law of Action must come into play in every scenario. Joining an online dating site, attending more events with friends, or finally agreeing to be fixed up on a blind date are some examples of doing that, which will, in turn, generate the motion or action. Having a keen sense of self and a solid connection to your higher self will also assist us in putting the Law of Action in motion. If you suddenly receive an intuitive hit or nudge that encourages you to take your dogs to the park, listen. By taking the dogs to the park, you are following the Law of Action, and through this initiative, you may meet the love of your life at that very park!

UNIVERSAL LAW #4—THE LAW OF CAUSE AND EFFECT

According to dictionary.com, one definition of cause-and-effect is "Noting a relationship between actions or events such that one or more are the result of the other or others."

The basis of the Law of Cause and Effect is karma. We reap what we sow. Every effect is a reaction to past actions and intentions. Creating our deeds and actions around the principles of positive words and behaviors leads to our receiving of positive words and behaviors. But then why is it that at times we receive the short end of the stick when, say, a random stranger is rude and unkind to us? That person has created a cause-and-effect ripple for themselves by which they will receive the same energy back from someone else. According to this law, every action has a wave created that affects something or someone else.

Alex is a young professional working at an accounting firm. He has always been a bit of a loner at work, keeping to himself and focusing solely on his tasks. Recently, he has been feeling unfulfilled, as though something is missing from his life. One day, while walking to lunch, Alex witnesses a colleague, Jamie, struggling to carry a heavy stack of documents. Despite his usual reserved nature, Alex decides to step outside of his proverbial box and help Jamie.

Alex's simple act of kindness—a smile and offering to carry half of the documents—leads to a conversation with Jamie. Jamie expresses gratitude and they start talking more, discovering shared interests. Over time, their friendship grows, and Jamie introduces Alex to a network of professionals and opportunities that Alex had been unaware of.

As Alex continues to help and support his colleagues and friends, he notices positive changes in his own life. He begins to feel more connected at work, finds new career opportunities, and gains a deeper sense of fulfillment from the relationships he builds. His acts of kindness ripple outward, creating a chain of positive effects in his professional and personal life.

Later, Alex reflects on how his initial decision to help Jamie set off a series of events that transformed his experience at work. He realizes that the Law of Cause and Effect, which states that every action has a corresponding reaction, was at play. By choosing to act with kindness, Alex's positive intentions created a series of beneficial outcomes, leading to growth and satisfaction in his life.

Through this experience, Alex understands that the energy and actions we put into the world come back to us in ways we might not always expect but can always appreciate. His journey demonstrates how the Law of Cause and Effect operates in everyday situations, showing that positive actions can lead to positive results.

I like to think of this law as a wave of ebb and flow, such as the rising and falling of sea levels, because the tide is the gravitational force of the moon and sun, as well as the rotation of the earth. The effects, therefore, are the high and low tides and the sea level. We can use this example to help immerse ourselves in the energy of the scales of balance. Every action triggers a chain of events.

One way to grasp the workings of this law is to be honest with ourselves about any areas in which we may subconsciously be creating an effect without consciously recognizing the cause. For example, in my practice as a psychic medium, many clients ask me why they have not yet been able to manifest a loving, kind, and faithful life partner, even after they have clearly written down all the particulars of their wants, wishes, and desires. After tuning in further to their auric fields for some of these clients, I can see the fear of intimacy or lack of faith that such a person with all these wonderful traits even exists! Can you see how the cause of these deep-seated fears has created an opposite effect from what they are trying to manifest?

To master this Spiritual Law, it enriches us to practice being kind and respectful to everyone we encounter. And it serves us to conduct our inner dialogues in the spirit of love, trust, faith, hope, and joy. Say this mantra every day: "I am worthy of respectful love" and watch the effects begin to manifest in your life!

Universal Law #5—The Law of Relativity

The word *relative* makes us contemplate how things are meaningful only as far as they relate to other things. Another definition of the word explains that relativity is a state of dependence in which the existence or significance of one entity is solely dependent on that of another. What does all this mean as it pertains to us individually and collectively?

The Law of Relativity holds that nothing is good or evil, right or wrong, hot or cold unless you compare or relate it to something else.

We will always be able to find people who are richer, thinner, kinder, less educated, poorer, or less talented than ourselves. The bell curve shows us that whatever our IQ may be, someone is always more or less intelligent than we are. The meaning or purpose we place on something is relative to how we perceive that very thing.

Imagine two psychics, Joan and Emma, who both offer spiritual readings. Joan feels discouraged because she sees Emma gaining more popularity and success in her practice. Joan starts to compare her abilities to Emma's, feeling like she is not as gifted or successful.

However, when Joan reflects on her own journey, she realizes that she has helped many people and has her own unique strengths. By recognizing that Emma's success does not diminish her own value, Joan understands that comparing herself to Emma is a matter of perspective.

In relation to a psychic who is just starting their practice, Joan is quite successful. Through the lens of the new psychic, Joan's accomplishments are something for which she would strive.

With the Law of Relativity, Joan comes to see that everyone's path is different, and that success and abilities are relative to individual experiences and contexts. This shift in perspective helps Joan appreciate her own achievements and find motivation in her own growth rather than focusing on Emma's success.

This is quite different from judging. You choose to employ a meaning or purpose to compare something in your life. We have each chosen life lessons or soul growth opportunities to experience in this lifetime.

Can you see how this Spiritual Law would, at first glance, appear to interfere with the Law of Attraction? After all, is everyone destined to have the perfect body (whatever that is!), and live in a multi-million-dollar beach house with a Ferrari parked out front, having won the Powerball lottery? Of course not! Everyone represents a different puzzle piece in this beautiful mystery of life. Some have unique shapes, with distinct colors, yet all are interwoven to complete the tapestry.

As with any other endeavor, the more we remember to use this law, the better our chance of mastering it. For example, we may choose to see the glass as half-full rather than half-empty. We can choose to focus on the good in any given situation. Think about how you choose to view your challenges. We can always spin a challenge into a positive outcome. It really is all simply a matter of intention and perception.

Everything is just what it is. It is as simple as that.

Universal Law #6—The Law of Polarity

Everything in our world is about balance. There cannot be an inside without an outside, an up without a down, a light without a dark. There is a continuum of counterparts and opposites. All that exists does so on a spectrum, and one aspect cannot exist without the other. There is a beautiful complementarity to every aspect of our lives.

If we never experienced pain, how could we deeply appreciate bliss and joy? Without experiences of hurt and disappointment in relationships, gratitude for a life partner who shares so much love and awareness would not be as strong. We have the free will to change our thoughts from one end of the spectrum to the other at any given time—even within the proverbial heartbeat.

At first glance, hot and cold appear to be opposites, yet upon further reflection, they are both aspects of the same thing: temperature. Yin and yang are polarizations of the other, yet both are essential. The very duality of the ease and complexity of this law gives us much to think about.

Suppose the Law of Attraction was always successful, and our lives were filled with only bliss, abundance, and joy. How could we benefit from soul-growth opportunities and the resulting expansion? We learn from our mistakes. We become better people after our "perceived failures." For me personally, I learned to love more deeply after experiencing the gut-wrenching pain of grief.

Jenna is a successful entrepreneur who runs a popular online business. While she loves her work, she often feels overwhelmed by the highs and lows of the revenue streams. When sales are high, she's thrilled, but when sales dip, she feels discouraged and anxious. One day, Jenna reads about the Spiritual Law of Polarity, which teaches that everything has two opposite poles and that both are necessary for growth and balance.

Jenna starts integrating the teachings of this Spiritual Law by acknowledging that the difficulties of her business are natural parts of the entrepreneurial journey. She realizes that success and failure are two poles of the same spectrum, and each offers valuable lessons. She begins to see that these extremes are not just challenges but opportunities for growth.

She begins to write about her feelings during successful periods and reflects on her responses during slower times. Through this practice of journaling, she learns to appreciate the lessons that come with both success and setbacks.

She begins a practice of gratitude and self-care during the slow times, knowing that these moments are necessary for her personal and professional development.

Jenna's understanding of the Law of Polarity transforms her approach to her business and life. She no longer fears the lows but instead sees them as opportunities for growth. She learns that by embracing both ends of the spectrum, she can achieve a more balanced and fulfilling entrepreneurial journey. Her newfound perspective allows her to manage her emotions better and make more informed decisions, leading to long-term success and personal satisfaction.

The way to harmony with this Spiritual Law is to learn balance and appreciate the challenge of the extremes with detachment. Within every disappointment is the potential for greatness. This law exists only in the physical realms. When you find the pendulum of your thoughts swinging toward the negative, stop, take a deep breath, and ask yourself, "What is the opposite of the emotion I am feeling?" If you are experiencing a feeling of worry and lack, shift your awareness to an energy of confidence and abundance.

UNIVERSAL LAW #7—THE LAW OF FREE WILL

Before incarnating into this lifetime, we made choices, including our parents, the particulars of soul contracts, and even the astrological energies of our date and time of birth. These choices involved discussion and input from our Spirit Guides and our consideration of areas in which we felt we needed more experience in the direction of expansion and growth.

During the life review and selection, past lives and karma also played a role in selecting our gender, the people who would play key roles in our lives, and the opportunities for lessons and the fulfillment of soul contracts we made to experience in this life.

The only time destiny or fate comes into play is when it is time for a soul contract or reunion to take place. Fate quietly directs us to be at the right place at the right time.

Since our Creator gave us the gift of free will, this is always in play. We can always choose a specific direction or outcome in our lives. We even have free-will choice when we leave our physical bodies and go to the other side. Our souls always have free will to either expand in our quest for enlightenment or to stagnate.

How does this Spiritual Law pertain to the Law of Attraction? If we agreed to a soul contract that said we would meet up with and marry someone from our soul group at a certain point, fate or destiny would bring that person across our paths. And let us say that our soul recognizes this person's soul immediately and knows that the two are to end up together. So, the one person who knows and is ready to move forward begins using the keys from the Law of Attraction to bring the other person to propose. The other person still has the gift of free will. And by using his or her free will, the choice can always be not to proceed with or honor the original soul contract. It could be that the naysayer has experienced too much pain and loss in a relationship and therefore suffers a lowered vibrational frequency. This, in turn, constricts the soul to such an extent that its frequency does not allow awareness of the original soul contract.

One way we can attempt to cooperate with this universal law fully is to recognize that the fulfillment of any wants, needs, and desires that we may be trying to draw to ourselves using the Law of Attraction, must not interfere with another's free will, or detract from their well-being.

UNIVERSAL LAW #8—THE LAW OF FAITH

This Spiritual Law teaches trust and surrender. According to Merriam-Webster, faith is belief in and trust in and loyalty to God, firm belief, even in the absence of proof.

When we step into the energy of lack of faith or distrust, we are allowing the fear of the ego mind to take control. This can often lead us down a deep, dark rabbit hole of despair. Then, the Law of Vibration steps onto the playing field, and the negative energy thus created vibrates around us and then out into the universe.

Who or what can we have faith in? Most people have faith in a God/Source/Creator, and their definitions or expressions of this entity vary from person to person and religion. While visiting the Other Side or the Spirit World, I saw that we all have a Spirit Team. This team comprises angels and guides always there when we call on them. As we enter a conscious relationship with our Spirit Team and learn to blend with their energy, it becomes easier to have faith in their role in our lives. A knowledgeable Spiritual Teacher will guide you on discovering and deepening your relationship with your Spirit Guides.

We also have the opportunity for openness to faith in ourselves. Can you begin to imagine how this task becomes easier the more inner personal work you do and the more you get to know who you are and what you are about? In time, a relationship forms with your Spirit Guides, and while discovering how to listen to their guidance, you in turn begin to have more faith in yourself.

How do we practice faith? Sometimes, it may feel like jumping off a cliff without knowing where you will land. But if you take this idea and turn it into a positive, there is an opportunity for enormous release within the act of free- falling. There is great beauty in the very process of trusting and surrendering.

Universal Law #9—The Law of Gender

This Spiritual Law teaches us that within both our inner and outer world, we have both masculine and feminine aspects. While transgender people may determine their gender, and sex may be assigned to an intersex baby, most of us incarnate as male or female. But almost all of us have experienced lifetimes as both male and female. Aided by our Spirit Guides, we make the gender decision for our upcoming lifetime during our life selection process.

When we fall out of balance to one extreme or another, the result is turmoil in our psyches. Judging another's process based on their choices creates an imbalance within our physical bodies. We must strive to embrace one another's freewill choices and lovingly support them on their journey to higher consciousness.

This Spiritual Law goes much deeper than the outward physical aspects of whether you represent yourself as male or female in this lifetime. This law supports the Law of Attraction in subtle ways. The more we go within and learn to utilize both aspects of our soul selves, the easier time we have in manifesting. The feminine aspects of ourselves assist us in creating and intuiting. However, the male aspects are also essential, as action requires the wheels of motion to turn toward manifestation.

The key to mastering this Universal Law is maintaining an equal balance of yin and yang, masculine and feminine. We are moving out of a male-dominated world and into a more divine feminine expression; however, we are striving for the perfect symbiotic interaction between the two. The more we experience this sacred merger, the closer we are to understanding the Law of Divine Oneness.

UNIVERSAL LAW #10—THE LAW OF DIVINE ONENESS

This is my personal favorite of the Spiritual Laws, for it resonates with the New Earth, the fifth dimension, the days of the Phoenix Rising. This Universal Law affirms that we are all one, and all connected to God Source, also referred to as Source. This law teaches us that the days of "I" and "me" are waning, and the days of "us" and "we" are birthed into a new era of Unity. We are all brothers and sisters.

In Chapter 8 we explore the concept of quantum entanglement. Quantum entanglement is a phenomenon in quantum physics where two or more particles become interconnected in such a way that the state of one particle instantly influences the state of another, regardless of the distance between them. This connection persists even when the particles are separated by vast distances, such that a change in the state of one particle instantly alters the state of the other.

The concept of quantum entanglement was introduced in 1935, however, it was not until the mid-80's and 90's that evidence of entanglement was proven through experiments. I love it when science catches up and proves the concepts conscious humans have known for millennium!

In Matthew 7:12, we are told "Do unto others as you would have them do unto you." If we strive to live our lives practicing the Golden Rule, and if we can remember that everything we think and do affects everyone and everything else, as we are all connected, then the overall vibration of the planet raises. The more we strive to honor this law, the more compassionate, understanding, and nonjudgmental we will be.

Why is it that it takes a tragedy for us all to come together in unity and help one another? Can you imagine a world in which neighbors help neighbors, cities help cities, and countries help countries? That world is now. The midwives of humanity stand waiting to give birth to this new paradigm.

Look for ways the Law of Oneness can guide you. Our goal as a soul is to realize enlightenment. We have a blessed opportunity within our physical bodies to assist our souls on this quest. Even a gesture as simple as an encouraging smile can alter the energy around us. Many people serve in a chain of charitable deeds known as "Pay It Forward." This works because when someone does something nice for you, you do something nice for them. Can you see how amazingly this process works, given that everything is energy? The ripple effect of this notion is mind-blowing, and very inspiring.

It may take humanity several more decades to fully embrace this Universal Law, but I can assure you, the energy of this law is upon us. It's up to you and me to embrace this law in our daily lives and breathe in the love energy of abundance for all, instead of the fear energy of lack. Let us sing the song of compassion and dance the dance of truth.

I hope you have gained a deeper understanding of the different Spiritual Laws and how their manifestations ebb and flow and work together. Learning to weave together the treasures from each law to work in synchronicity with each other provides us with the greatest gifts.

INVITATION TO EXPLORE

Take time to journal about areas in your life where you can use the Universal or Spiritual Laws. Think about instances in which the Law of Attraction was not successful for you and write about some reasons using examples from some of the other spiritual laws discussed in this chapter.

CHAPTER 5

THE WEB OF DESTINY: UNDERSTANDING PAST LIVES AND SOUL CONTRACTS

PAST LIVES AND SOUL CONTRACTS

Have you ever experienced déjà vu when you visited a city that was new to you? Perhaps you felt a sense of belonging and knowing, yet you had never been there. It is quite common to have these feelings when you are somewhere in this lifetime that you are familiar with from a past life. There is no logical explanation for the emotions you feel, yet you know with all certainty that you *know* this place.

Some people have vivid dreams of their past lives and can clearly remember the details. Upon waking from these dreams, the dreamer knows that he or she was reliving an experience from another time and place. Past-life dreams are much different from ordinary dreams. Often, we are shown the particulars of places we have never even thought about. Yet these scenes are quite true to the time and place.

The general belief in past lives has increased significantly over the years, partly because of the success of books about reincarnation. Brian Weiss, M.D., a Columbia- and Yale-trained psychiatrist, was initially a skeptic himself. In his best-selling book *Many Lives, Many Masters*, Dr. Weiss shares the experience of one of his patients, Catherine, who, under hypnosis, relived events from her past life. Remarkably, Catherine could also channel messages from "the space between lives," which contained remarkable revelations about Dr. Weiss's family and his deceased son. This book has transformed the lives of countless readers, and is one of those "must reads" anyone on a spiritual journey.

There are children who are born knowing and remembering one or more of their past lives. James Leininger is one of those children. James began providing details from his past life as navy fighter pilot James M. Huston Jr. at the tender age of two. The specifics little James could provide were amazing, including names, places, and very particular details he had no way of knowing. If this story fascinates you, check out the book Bruce and Andrea Leininger wrote called *Soul Survivor: The Reincarnation of a World War II Fighter Pilot* about their son's accounts of his life as Lt Huston, killed in the Battle of Iwo Jima—over seventy years ago!

I have been shown in meditation, as well as when I visit the other side during mediumship readings, that before each of our incarnations , we go through a process called Life Preview, in which we meet with our Guides to discuss what we would like to achieve or work on during the upcoming lifetime. Michael Newton also writes about this in his amazing book *Journey of Souls*. If you have not read this book, I highly recommend it. Using a special hypnosis technique to reach the hidden memories of subjects, Dr. Newton unveiled amazing insights into what happens to us between lives. *Journey of Souls* is the record of 29 people who recalled their experiences between physical deaths.

Our souls choose to continue the growth and expansion process through reincarnation. According to Webster, reincarnation is "rebirth in new bodies or forms of life; especially a soul's rebirth in a new human body. The soul's quest is for advancement, growth, and enlightenment. Part of the way to realize this is to experience varied lifetimes. As previously noted, in some lifetimes, we choose a male body; in others, we choose a female body. Planet Earth is in a third-dimensional frequency now. To choose an incarnation on this planet is both a blessing and a challenge. It is a blessing because of the unbelievable beauty we can experience on Mother Earth. We can share our love both physically and emotionally. The gifts this planet offers us are endless. Yet, due to the density of our Earth, there are many challenges—also known as difficulties—to work through and overcome. Since we each have free will, Earth is where we can incarnate to balance our karma and work for soul growth and refinement.

During these life previews, we collaborate with our Spirit Guides to make appropriate choices based on experiences from our past lives. In addition to gender, examples of the choices we make include race and nationality, country and geography, physical characteristics, who our parents will be, and the opportunities for soul growth we will be presented with.

When we go through what is akin to a brainstorming session with our Spirit Guides, what are they going to be assisting us with? In reviewing many of our past lives, they will offer insight on ways we can balance the karma from our past lives while expanding the soul simultaneously.

Among our soul-growth opportunities, we may choose to work on issues related to concepts of money—from poverty to abundance. We may decide to experience certain health challenges. We may choose to teach or increase awareness of societal issues. Or as in my case, we may choose not to have biological children. As I discussed in Chapter 4 on additional Spiritual Laws, our souls have free will. Free will is the ability to decide which circumstances, among infinite possibilities, we will experience. As humans, we all possess this freedom. The energy of any challenging—and seemingly negative—lessons set by the soul before incarnating cannot typically be avoided by mere displays of positivity. Only acceptance, full understanding, and forgiveness can do that.

I have also learned that our Spirit Team or Spirit Guides will assist us if we ask them to, but they will *not* assist in bringing about something that clearly goes against what our soul's wish was prior to being born. They were there and helped us make these choices, so they will certainly not betray our soul's choice of growth opportunity.

As a further example of this, we will use a fictional character named Ruth. When Ruth participated in her life preview, her Spirit Guides lovingly pointed out many lifetimes in which Ruth was extremely wealthy. Yet, she used her money and power against others and even allowed people around her to die of hunger instead of sharing her wealth. In most of Ruth's past lives, she had been given opportunities to learn the lesson of charitable giving, yet in every life, she chose greed and gluttony over philanthropic gestures. For her most recent life, Ruth had chosen, of her own free will, to experience periods of hardship that would require assistance from others. More than likely, in Ruth's current lifetime, no matter how many tools from *The Secret* she uses, she will not win the Powerball. Does this mean Ruth will always be poverty-stricken in this current lifetime? No, it does not. However, her soul chose to experience the karma she had inflicted on others in many of her past lives.

Through training in past-life regression in beautiful Sedona, Arizona, led by a woman I consider to be an Earth Angel, Mary

Elizabeth Raines (Rainey to her students), I was shown many of my lifetimes where I had not been "the best parent," so to speak. In many of these incarnations, I was a father who left his young children for one reason or another. Many times, I was a mother, who put other things before raising her children. It was finally beginning to make sense why I would not have children during this incarnation, no matter how much I tried to manifest it! This was not done to punish me for the past lifetimes; rather, this was chosen by my soul to balance certain karma that required balancing for my soul growth. All my questions were answered once this realization came through and any self-doubt released! Finally, I was freed from my perceived "manifestation failure!"

By its very nature, the soul desires expansion. With expansion comes wisdom, and the ability to more or less shed the ego. We, as a soul, strive to reach a state of enlightenment during each incarnation. What does it mean to become enlightened? One of the more worldly definitions of enlightenment is education, which results in understanding and increased knowledge. I resonate with the belief that growing awareness not only improves our insight into many areas but also opens our souls to greater consciousness. Buddhists consider enlightenment as the state that transcends the wheel of rebirth and is characterized by the absence of the desire and suffering of individual consciousness.

What do past lives have to do with manifesting? Well, they play a significant role in what we can manifest and what we are not able to manifest. So, if you have been unable to manifest something you truly felt you desired, it may benefit you to schedule a past-life regression. It is especially important to check the background and training of the regression therapist you choose to work with. Find out where they received their training. Read testimonials to their work or ask friends for recommendations.

There are also psychics and Akashic record readers who specialize in past-life readings. As a psychic medium that places immense value on ethics, accuracy, and validation, this is an area or modality for which I recommend a great deal of caution and research. An unethical psychic could very easily weave together a tapestry of untruths regarding your past lives. Ensure you get a recommendation from someone you trust, and then check out their experience, credentials, and testimonials. Past lives, karma, and the choices our souls make from lifetime to lifetime are issues that are too important to take lightly.

For me, it was the combined results from a past-life reading and many past-life regressions that led me to the realization of why my soul had chosen not to bear children during this lifetime.

I have found it is human nature to beat ourselves up when we cannot manifest something especially important to us. It may weigh heavily on our hearts, minds, and souls for years— sometimes seemingly forever. This should not be. Many inner knowing's are revealed when we learn to use the tools provided to us by our Creator and Spirit Guides. When these realizations dawn, they open a clearing where our gifts may shine, and our life purpose or soul path is clear. When we are not saddled with grief and sadness, and we can reach the point of complete release, our lives begin to open in ways we could not have imagined.

SOUL GROUPS AND SOUL TRIBES

Have you, or another family member, been called the black sheep of your family? Do people joke around, that you, or they, must have been adopted or that the stork dropped you off at the wrong house? If this resonates with you, you may have chosen to incarnate into a family that is not part of your soul group.

Souls reside in pods or groups, where each soul reincarnates with members of their group and surrounding groups throughout many lifetimes. Each soul group normally has between eight and fifteen members. Then other soul groups are connected to your soul group. My Spirit Team has shown me the best way to describe this is to imagine oval pods connected by an etheric cord. Each oval pod contains souls within that soul group. Yet souls from one pod may choose to incarnate with a soul from a neighboring pod if both souls agree they would be a good fit to help each other with their soul growth or to resolve karmic issues.

Sometimes, members of a soul group are quite different from members of your biological family. Sometimes, a soul will choose to incarnate into a family not part of their soul pod to gain knowledge, wisdom, and opportunities for soul growth. If you have chosen to incarnate with someone who causes you great personal struggle and difficulty, this is a sign you are an old soul. A young or new soul would not choose something this challenging.

Souls from our soul groups or tribes incarnate with us in numerous ways in different lifetimes. We each have a group of souls in our group, and I have seen in meditation that we share lifetimes with souls from our immediate group as well as connecting soul groups. For instance, your husband may have incarnated in a past life as your brother or father. Or a soul from a neighboring soul group may agree to incarnate during a specific lifetime as your mother to assist you in resolving certain matters in your life that have previously challenged you. In this case, you may not feel the same close bond with your mother in that lifetime as you would if a soul from your immediate soul group had incarnated as your mother.

I have given many readings in which a person asked me about their relationship, and when I tune in, I am shown a recent past life as siblings. The person I am reading for will exclaim, "I'm always telling my friends that my husband feels more like a big brother than a husband!" When this happens, there is a soul memory of the lifetime as brother and sister. These are not the best ingredients for an intimate sexual relationship. Does this mean the relationship is doomed? Not at all. In these instances, I recommend that one or preferably both spouses have past-life regressions to "clear" the soul memory of the lifetime when their spouse was their sibling. Another beneficial tool is to find an experienced life coach, Akashic record reader, or intuitive counselor who can assist in locating the soul contract between the husband and the wife. Was there a soul contract showing that they had chosen to experience a lifetime as spouses even though they had been siblings in the most recent past life? If there were indeed a soul contract, this would provide more information for the couple to proceed normally, assuming they choose to remain together.

Many times, souls from a soul group may meet up later in life when each member's energetic vibration has molded itself into a more uniform pattern. When this occurs, there is a feeling of instant knowing, instant recognition, and overall love. There is great beauty in having another person truly recognize your soul and see you for who you are.

A soul tribe is different from a soul group. You can be part of a soul tribe without being in the same soul group as its members. The nature of a soul tribe is to join forces for a common cause. The members of your soul tribe understand you and share the same belief systems you do.

When we meet other members of our soul tribes, a new energetic vibration forms A frequency is created by the joining together of two or more souls with similar soul contracts. With this new frequency comes an opportunity for each member to help other members tune in to their soul's purpose as individuals and as a group. We will delve deeper into life or soul purpose in the next chapter.

Another beautiful aspect of meeting the members of your soul tribe is that the divine design behind you connecting with this group is normally for a collective purpose. Perhaps you each have a passion for animal welfare, or environmental issues. Maybe you all have studied energy healing and choose to form a collective. Perhaps you are all psychics and enjoy the camaraderie. Still, another group may join forces in communal housing. The options are endless. The key is to watch for synchronicities and signs. Start the dialogue. Our Spirit Team is here to help us! All we need to do is ask.

Sometimes, members of our soul tribes do not live close to us. The advent of the Internet has allowed us to participate in our soul tribes all over the world. You may find that members of your soul tribe often live far away or even in another country.

At times, we are members of more than one soul tribe. There is nothing more exciting than meeting members of our soul tribes! A feeling of appreciation and gratitude tends to envelop our energy fields. There is never an atmosphere of competition within a true soul tribe. It is just the opposite. Members within a soul tribe strongly desire to lift each other. There is a yearning to help your fellow soul tribe members achieve every success, joy, and accomplishment their soul aspires to.

If you have not yet found your soul tribe, what are things you can do to connect with them?

First, be aware that your tribe is already waiting for you. Be sure to set the intention and talk to your Spirit Team. Let them know you have learned what you needed to learn from your biological family and ask for the energy to send out the signals to connect with your soul tribe.

Second, strive for a deep understanding of yourself and your main interests. Make a list of all that you are enthusiastic about. Once you have identified your passions, form a group, or join an existing group focusing on the issues you are enthusiastic about.

The more emotional work you have done on yourself, the more likely you will connect with your soul tribe. This process is not about ego. It is the exact opposite of ego. It is about getting to know your true self, your soul self, and remembering what you came here to accomplish. Finding our soul tribe often coincides with truly "finding" ourselves.

This chapter would not be complete without emphasis on karma. Given that karma corresponds to the Spiritual Law of Cause and Effect and that the wheel of karma is always turning, would it not make sense to focus on harmony, as well as contributing to the well-being of our fellow sentient beings? Avoid falling into the trap of evading responsibility for your life by making excuses or playing the victim. Be mindful, too, that assistance and sharing come in different forms. Giving someone a sincere compliment costs nothing! Sharing a smile with a stranger does not affect your bank balance, yet the ripple effect can change lives. Let us do our part in creating a world where everyone makes generous deposits to their karmic bank account daily!

INVITATION TO EXPLORE

Consider finding a certified past-life regression counselor and making an appointment. Reviewing our past lives can often shed light on areas in our current lives where we may be experiencing struggles. Past-life sessions are normally quite healing and enlightening!

Journal about the characteristics of those who will be part of your soul tribe. Have you met any tribal members yet? If not, journal about the passions and interests that you expect these people will share with you.

CHAPTER 6

YOUR DIVINE BLUEPRINT: UNCOVERING YOUR SOUL'S PATH AND PURPOSE

At some point in our lives, we ask existential questions such as "Why am I here?," "What did I agree to accomplish in this lifetime?" and "What are my talents, and what am I meant to do?"

At various stages of our lives, we wonder what direction we are supposed to go in. We are curious about our spiritual (or life) path and what has been divinely orchestrated for us.

As discussed in a previous chapter, before incarnating, we go to what many of Dr. Michael Newton's hypnosis patients refer to as The Ring of Destiny. Our souls go to this room where we can preview our next life choices. Once our guides and council help us make a decision , the major lessons we are to learn in the next life are set in the form of soul contracts.

This is where the concept of the Law of Attraction appears not to always function as a complementary Spiritual Law. For instance, if we attempt to manifest a lottery win and have chosen to learn the lesson of poverty or financial challenges, we will probably not win the lottery. If we attempt to manifest having children, and we have chosen to learn lessons from being barren, more than likely, we will not have children. This does not mean that efforts at manifestation do not work! Most of the time, they do work. However, there are other Spiritual Laws that work in conjunction with the Law of Attraction.

Most people have multiple missions and life paths. These missions become apparent at certain ages or periods of our lives. And at other times, the missions may overlap. It is important to determine whether something you are passionate about is part of your primary life path or is more of a secondary or ancillary mission. For me, there was a time when I was torn about whether my life path would be as a medium and spiritual teacher, or as an activist for animal welfare. After reflection and contemplation, I realized that primarily, I came here to be an evidential medium, psychic channel and spiritual teacher for many. This does not mean that I view my responsibility to advocate for animals less seriously than I ever have. It simply means that others choose a primary life path of animal rescue, welfare, and activism. I can still contribute to these endeavors through volunteer work and trying to educate others about the soul nature of all sentient beings.

Where do we begin to discover our life path or mission? The first thing is to really get to know ourselves inside and out. Consider what you like and dislike, as well as what your strengths and weaknesses are. Just because we are proficient in a certain area, does not mean this is meant to be our life purpose.

For example, my college degree is in business administration. After I moved to Southern California, I sat for the CPA (certified public accountant) exam and passed it on the first attempt, which is highly unusual. I managed a business management entertainment CPA firm in the Los Angeles area for several years. I then decided to open my own firm, which proved quite successful. I employed several people and had many clients from all over the country. However, as mentioned earlier, I became quite sick and almost died.

I am an excellent CPA and money manager. I earned a great deal of money in that career. Yet, it is not my life path or life mission. It is not what I "signed up" to accomplish. This does not mean that others cannot find meaning in walking the life path of a CPA or money manager. Of course, they can. Do I regret all the years I spent studying and building my business? No, it made me who I am, and the experience I acquired helps me during intuitive business sessions with my clients. It also helps me manage my business more efficiently.

I wanted to share more about my journey so that others may be inspired to look at their own lives and be moved to moments of deep reflection. If you have tried to manifest a certain career path only to be faced with hurdle after hurdle or obstacle after obstacle, perhaps this is the universe's way of gently nudging you in another direction. Or perhaps you continue to get sick when you try to remain in a job or career that is not part of your life path.

A helpful tool to use for life-path guidance is the life path number. To calculate your personal life path number, add up all the numbers in your date of birth. I will use my mom's birthday as an example. She was born July 25, 1944. You add up all the digits: $7 + 2 + 5 + 1 + 9 + 4 + 4 = 32$; then you continue adding until you have a single digit: $3 + 2 = 5$. My mom's life path number was a five. A 5-life path number represents people who are flexible, adaptable, and enjoy new environments. People with a 5-life path also make great counselors. This really suited my mom as she was known as a gypsy, moving more times than anyone I know! She craved new experiences and was an amazing person to mediate disputes, as she could easily see both sides of any situation.

There are entire books and courses on life path numbers and numerology, but for this book, I will offer a quick reference to each life path number.

Life path 1—These individuals are born leaders and innovators. Potential careers for life path one people are entrepreneur, manager, politician, and senior managers.

Life path 2—People on this life path pay attention to details, enjoy balance and equilibrium, and are inclined toward the mystic. Writers, artists, meditators, psychics, and child psychologists are commonly found on life path two.

Life path 3—My life path —My life path number is a three. This path is all about creativity and helping others. It is a highly empathetic number on a mission to inspire and uplift others. Publishing and media fit into this category. A preponderance of actors, artists, writers, public speakers, and psychics share this life path number.

Life path 4—This life path number is associated with security, responsibility, and plain challenging work. Family and legacy are important to the life path four people. Accountants, bankers, financial planners, engineers, architects, real estate moguls, and tax lawyers may all fit in this category.

Life path 5—As in the case of my mother, life path number 5 represents people who are flexible, adaptable, and eager to experience new environments. Those along this path tend to dislike routine and prefer jobs and careers involving travel or the outdoors. Counselors, firefighters, construction workers, and those who must travel in their careers are often among the fives.

Life path 6—These individuals' paths are about peace, harmony, and healing, as well as a connection to music and/or art. They are also great nurturers and intuitive. They have an affinity with children and animals. Their life path professions may include teacher, healer, writer, artist, and interior decorator.

Life path 7—People on path seven are misunderstood at times, as they prefer the mysterious and may require a great deal of alone time. This desire for solitude may facilitate connection to higher realms if the person learns to meditate and tune in properly. Sevens are analytical people and highly intelligent. A mathematician, chemist, detective, doctor, psychic channel, or scientist would all be great choices for a life path seven.

Life Path 8—Individuals born under the influence of Life Path 8 normally make great leaders. They are also able to manage large sums of money. They have an affinity for power, and their business skills are usually outstanding. Career options would include business leader, accountant, financial advisor, and high-ranking law enforcement officer.

Life Path 9—Guiding and inspiring people born under Life Path 9 is a great deal of idealism. Most are old souls who chose to incarnate to help humanity somehow. Many are natural-born volunteers and humanitarians. Mother Teresa was a life path nine. Social work, teaching, diplomacy, and intuitive counseling would all be good career choices for a life path nine.

If numerology interests you, you can find books written on the subject. I am certainly not a numerologist; however, I very much resonate with the accuracy of the information that comes from working with numerology. This description barely scratches the surface of this ancient esoteric modality.

There are spiritual practitioners who find themselves called to assist people in discovering their true path. Some people benefit from past-life regression or even life-between-life regression, as the sessions prove beneficial in determining our souls' challenges and progress. According to The Newton Institute, a life-between-life session is a deep hypnotic process developed over many years, designed to heighten awareness of one's soul self and Spirit Guides, thereby awakening an understanding of immortal identity. Many people have received great insight from participating in these regressions. I have benefited from them, with past-life regression training and certification guiding me ever deeper.

The more we tune in and get to know our authentic soul selves, the more easily we can access and remember our life mission for this lifetime. Studying intuitive development with a qualified teacher assists people in getting to know themselves better. One of my missions in this lifetime is as a spiritual teacher. I created an online academy, Intuitive Compass Academy, so that anyone located anywhere in the world could participate in my classes. I cannot tell you how many of my students over the years were finally ready to step into the energy of who they are and what they came here to do. I also created an in-person academy, Mississippi Academy for Psychic and Mediumship Studies, and people are traveling from all over the country to attend. Other seers have told me that I am a catalyst of sorts, to promote and assist others on their journey.

My work is another example of paying attention to signs from the universe. I had absolutely no plans or intention to teach intuitive psychic development. None whatsoever. Many years after becoming a professional psychic, some clients started asking me to teach them about intuition. I smiled and went on with my day. Remember, one of my Spirit Guides talks about me sometimes needing to be hit over the head with an etheric two-by-four before I pay attention! After a period of time and many, many requests, I started thinking about developing a program. Mind you, I was still simply *thinking* about it! And then, I was at an event with other colleagues, and Marc Lainhart, a fellow Best American Psychic colleague, handed me a polished crystal rock with the word's "teacher" written on it! OK, the message finally sunk in! I began writing the course material and scheduled my first class. I am so grateful for the gentle and not-so-gentle nudges along the way.

Looking back, I now recognize that my higher self always tried to tell me I am a teacher. When other kids my age were playing with Barbies and baby dolls, or even playing doctor, I was playing teacher. I had a chalkboard lined up with all my stuffed animals for their lessons. Nothing like having a captive audience full of stuffed bears, dogs, and bunnies! All joking aside, can you see how my nine-year-old self was already "in the know" about one of my soul contracts? Think back to your childhood and see if there were any clues about your life path.

At times, I have had clients tell me they believe they are too old to change directions. We are *never* too old to adjust our path! Some of us need to have had experiences preparatory to taking the steps toward our life purpose. Others may have to honor multiple soul contracts, tailored to various chapters of their lives. And then there are those of us who require many signs and synchronicities, or even the extreme of a near-death experience before we alter the direction of our lives. Whatever your personal circumstances, it is important not to beat yourself up or harbor regrets. Every encounter and event in our lives happens to help our souls expand. Knowledge and wisdom from our past provide an endless stream of power that expands our awareness.

The serene confidence that comes from following your calling is eloquently beautiful. By sad contrast, the static frustration of those who choose to avoid the risks involved in pursuing their hunches and ideas is painful to behold.

Great benefit is in store when we explore our dark or shadow side. It was psychiatrist Carl Jung who named our dark side the *shadow*. According to Wikipedia, the shadow may refer to (1) an unconscious aspect of the personality that the conscious ego does not identify or (2) the entirety of the unconscious, i.e., everything of which a person is not fully conscious. In short, the shadow is the "dark side." To truly know oneself, we must recognize and own the dark side of ourselves and the bright side. Again, this goes back to the Law of Polarity, which we discussed in Chapter 4. According to Jung, "That which we do not bring to consciousness appears in our lives as fate." In a talk about accepting the darkness in self and others, Alan Watts explained: "Jung taught that the task in life, which thus confronts everyone, is to become conscious of and integrate one's shadow into one's conscious personality, accepting it with open arms not as an abhorrent aspect of one's self, but as a necessary and vital part of one's being." Getting to know our shadow selves propels us to realize our goals. There are amazing books to read and courses to take that help us work with our shadow side. Moment-to-moment inquiry into our true motives is especially helpful.

Now is a perfect time to talk about trust and surrender. We looked at trust in Chapter 4, in the section about the Law of Faith. What is trust? According to one definition, it is "a firm belief in the reliability, truth, ability, or strength of someone or something." In what or in whom do you have trust? Do you trust yourself? Do you trust that there is a higher power or God or Source? What about your Spirit Guides? Do you trust that you have personal Spirit Guides always there to guide you? As I have mentioned several times, I love teaching intuitive development and helping people understand the role of their Spirit Team, as well as acquainting them with their guides and higher self. Vast resources of wisdom and knowledge are available from our all-loving guides.

This is where surrender enters the mix. Merriam-Webster tells us that one definition of surrender is to give up completely. I know that for myself and many of you, control is one of life's toughest lessons. To be in control gives us a feeling of invulnerability and power. At times, it may even seem like a drug, in that you may struggle with actual withdrawal symptoms when you feel you are losing that control. I have learned that we are rarely in control of anything other than our free will.

When we try to control another person, it normally backfires on us. At this point, we can still stop, back up, take a breath, and understand that even though we may have succeeded in controlling that person, it is always a lose-lose situation of the jailer and jailed. Neither person has gained anything.

What about when we try to use control to navigate the path of our lives? How has that worked out for you? I know for myself, not so well. For years, I was under the false assumption that if you had a desire or an accomplishment you yearned to achieve, the best way to succeed was to plow forward, full steam ahead! I was so heavily addicted to my *drug* of control that I often failed to see the caution signs along the way. Looking back, I remember times when the red light signaling me to STOP flashed so brightly, it was probably seen in outer space! Yet, I raced forward at lightning speed, missing the signs and signals from my Spirit Team that should have been obvious. Have you endured similar dynamics in your life? Are you currently plowing forward so quickly and aggressively that you are missing key signs or landmarks along the way?

Let's play a game together. Let's celebrate the fact that you have just won the Powerball lottery. Congrats! Once the partying has died down, take time to journal about the things you intend to buy. Will you be getting things for your friends and family? What will you buy? Are you going to quit your job? How and when will you notify your bosses? Do you think you might start a business? If so, what type? Are you interested in devoting your now-free time to volunteer work? If so, what type speaks to you?

Your lottery journaling will reveal much about who and what is near and dear to your heart. Some of your answers will unambiguously show how important your current job is to you. If the first response out of your conscious mind was, "Hell, yeah! That job is history!" This tells you that your current work does not resonate with your life purpose. Or you may be in the correct field but simply with the wrong company. Do not wait to win the lottery to make these changes! In the words of Joseph Campbell, "Follow your bliss!"

If you get excited thinking about a certain business, you would buy or start, let this be a key to unlocking your soul's hidden passions. Begin researching the business and start writing a business plan. Sometimes, the very act of writing a plan either attracts the energy of the business to inform and invigorate your life sooner than anticipated, or it shows you a different direction that is more beneficial to you.

Have you thought about volunteer work or charities you would love to be more actively involved in? Contact these non-profits and ask what they need. See if any of their needs fit in with your current schedule. Some people love animals but do not have time to devote to caring for them full-time. I know people in this situation who contribute their time driving the animals to other areas, so they will have greater chances for adoption! Can you see this is an important part of the wheel?

These exercises will illuminate your life path and expedite your journey. When this lifetime is complete, what do you wish to be remembered for? What would you like your legacy to be?

The key to evolutionary strides along your life path is to really get in touch with your soul and surrender, so that events may unfold as they are supposed to. I encourage each of you to continue the practice of manifestation in your lives, while also learning to surrender to your soul's master plan.

INVITATION TO EXPLORE

Read a book on the shadow self or find a course that helps you explore your shadow. Consider studying intuitive development through courses or books. Using your life path number, deepen your understanding of its energies by reading books and watching YouTube presentations about numerology. Research certified past-life and/ or between-life therapists with the goal of further discovering your life path. Spend time considering the "lottery game" we just played and journal about your results.

CHAPTER 7

MANIFESTING IN THE QUANTUM

Everything is comprised of energy or waves, including human beings. Quantum physics teaches us that everything is energy, including people, animals, trees, rocks, and even water. We are not just our physical bodies. We also have an etheric body, an emotional body, a mental body, and an astral body. Our thought patterns, words, and even actions affect our energy vibration. As mentioned in chapter 5, past-life memory as well as events from earlier in our lives can affect our energetic signature.

I have discovered through experience that it is much more complicated to discover your life path or soul essence when your energy field is low or vibrating at a low frequency. This is a complex subject, so for the purposes of the concepts in this book, I am going to focus on tools to help increase your frequency.

Thought patterns create a wave or frequency that ripples out from your energy field. Strive to generate ideas and beliefs that increase your vibrational frequency, as well as that of the people around you. As we walk confidently toward the fifth dimension of the New Earth, we need to remember that each of us vibrates as part of a collective. In the next chapter, we will discuss this in depth. The focus of this chapter is to set your intentions to keep your frequency elevated to assist Gaia in her ascension while also raising the collective consciousness.

Positive thinking is a process that leads your mind to embrace joy, happiness, success, and positive results. We are inherently predisposed to surround ourselves with positive-thinking individuals. Just being in a positive-thinking individual's energy can uplift our energy.

Those who think negatively teach their minds to accept fear, worry, unhappiness, and negative results or outcomes. My husband, Daniel, ever bringing humor into the mix, loves to remind people not to use stinkin' thinkin,' as this contributes to our energy vibrating at the lower end of the frequency spectrum. Zig Ziglar, who preceded Tony Robbins as a motivational speaker, originally coined the phrase *stinking thinking* in his seminars. He taught that stinking thinking did not provide the right formula for manifesting good things.

There are many ways we can self-sabotage by allowing in the negative self-talk. One example of negative thinking and programming is when we use the word *always* or *never* to describe a situation that we have encountered. For example, let's say that Julie is turned down for a job position she applied for. The negative way to express this disappointment would be for Julie to say, "I'm never hired for the jobs I want," or "They always choose someone else for the position I really wanted." What would be the wiser choice of words in this situation? Julie could say, "I'm disappointed that someone else was chosen for the position; however, I trust that the Universe has my back and has something even better in store for me!"

Negative thought patterns may also run amuck when we verbalize regretful feelings—*I shoulda, woulda*, and *coulda*. The energy of regret can be a hazardous road to travel. What is regret? Regret is fervently wishing you had done something differently. Life continually presents us with choices. We may choose to act and pursue an opportunity or to ignore or reject the opportunity. Some blithely jump from an airplane without considering whether they have a parachute to help in their descent.

Conversely, some shy away from opportunities due to fear—fear of failure, fear of rejection, fear of disappointment, etc. They may live with the proverbial deer-in-the-headlights look deeply etched on their faces. I have found the highest-vibrational decision arises from the spectrum between these two extremes. When we tune in to an opportunity while in the greatest alignment with our Higher Selves, we receive proper clarity on whether to jump. Trust me on this! When we are in that space of trust, flow, and ease, the Universe will not allow us to jump without our parachutes!

We need to remember that, as imperfect humans, we will sometimes make decisions while we are not in perfect alignment. At such times, it is imperative that we not buy in to the energy and notion of regret. Regret takes us out of the now and into the nonexistent fruitlessness of *woulda, coulda,* and *shoulda*. Regret takes us down a dark road of guilt and shame. Guilt and shame work tirelessly to keep our energy hovering at the lower end of the frequency spectrum. What we can do, however, is learn from our mistakes. We can choose to work through our limiting beliefs and fears. We can embrace change and new opportunities if we know deep in our soul that we are not being reckless in our behaviors.

Be incredibly careful about labeling yourself or others in less-than-flattering terms such as stupid, loser, broke, unlucky, or fat, even if you say these words jokingly or in jest. Many times, when I have lovingly pointed out to someone that they are using lower-vibrational words, the response will be, "I'm just joking around." The Universe records every thought, word, phrase, and action. No disclaimer of comedy will stop the Universe from recording every word you say!

I even invite you to change the way you say, "I'm sorry." Putting that energy out into the Universe is not in your best interest! What is the definition of sorry? *Sorry* has the connotation of being worthless, and creates an energy of regret, the negative influence we have already discussed. Try to get in the habit of saying "I apologize" instead of "I'm sorry." This may seem silly, but I promise that you will notice a shift in your energy field when you begin making these slight changes in the words you choose.

People can easily become addicted to negative thought patterns and negative words. As we progress along the path to ascension, we find ourselves unable to be in the company of these types of individuals for extended periods, if at all. They are toxic to our physical, emotional, and spiritual well-being.

Most of us accept these concepts, as we live in the third-dimensional earth plane. The key is to make a point of practicing positive thinking in your daily life. Find affirmations that appeal to you and practice saying them aloud every morning before you begin your day. Examples are, "I am blessed," "I am pure love," "I am abundant," "I am grateful for all the divine opportunities the Universe provides me."

All living beings are affected by the energy of their environment; however, those who have chosen to become aware and raise their energetic vibration are even more affected. It is vital for those on a spiritual path to be in an environment geared to emotional protection and relaxation. I make sure to tell my students that as they walk through the doors of expansion, awareness, and awakening, they can never turn back. Expanding our awareness changes our frequency in an incredibly positive way. However, I would be remiss in not explaining the changes that occur with the choice to awaken.

The environment is critical to those who walk the path of expansion and awareness. Pre-awakening, you may be able to tolerate low-vibrational people and environments. Post-awakening, being in the energy of low-vibrational people can be pure torture on the auric field. It is important that we not stand in judgment of those who have not awakened or who still choose lower-vibrational words, actions, and lifestyles. It is certainly not our place to judge. But it is our responsibility to exercise discernment and to walk away from these toxic people and environments with love and grace.

All energy can be balanced with positive thinking, which raises your vibrational level, and working with a qualified energy practitioner to release past trauma. This, however, is an ongoing, lifelong challenge, so be gentle and loving with your evolvement over time.

As we follow these concepts and learn to honor our connection to Source, our energy vibrates at a higher frequency. Another wonderful way to increase our vibration is to embrace the concept of Unity and Divine Consciousness instead of the more common notion of separateness and division. We are all One and part of Source. I will discuss this concept in detail in the next chapter. When we practice unconditional love, joy, acceptance, compassion, and tolerance, we, in turn, raise our vibrational frequency, as we are all connected.

After you have successfully raised your vibration, you will notice profound change in many areas of your life. I am enthusiastic about discussing all the positive changes that occur when our frequency rises.

CONTROL

When we raise our vibrational frequency, our need to control everything that happens is diminished. If you stop and think about this, you will see that control takes a great deal of time and energy. And it's certainly not a sexy word! The ego mind governs fear, which in turn limits outcomes. Control is dominated and directed by fear. By contrast, surrender allows for limitless possibilities. Surrendering requires absolute faith in ourselves, our Spirit Team, God/Goddess, and the Spiritual Laws of the Universe. This is not always the easiest path to navigate. But if we train our minds to focus on the fact that we are indeed co-creators of our Universe and our lives, this empowers us to embrace the ease and flow of allowing the Divine to beautifully orchestrate the highest and best outcome in everything we do. Breathe in the energy of this for a moment. Feel it in the depths of your soul. Trusting to the point of surrender is one of the greatest gifts you can give to yourself.

JOY

When we offer positive words, thoughts, and actions, we experience joy more frequently. Other words for joy are delight, ebullience, elation, and happiness. These are such light, fun words. When I ponder the emotion of joy, I am made aware that many times humans feel guilty when they experience true joy or bliss. Why is this? If someone has been made to feel unworthy, the radio dial in their minds may be stuck on the station that tells them they don't deserve joy. Or maybe they play the station that warns them that when good things happen, the other shoe will surely drop soon. Or possibly, being depressed and down all the time has brought them more attention. Practice being in a state of joy. Make time to play. Of the thousands of readings I have done, one of the main messages from our loved ones on the other side is this: "Have fun! Play more!" Most children have not been programmed to question or abandon their joy. We can learn a lot from children. What I can tell you is this: The more you focus on raising your vibration, the more comfortable you will be wearing the bright attire of joy.

ENVIRONMENT

When you raise your vibrational frequency, you notice that you need more quiet and alone time and simply cannot be in certain places where you used to go. My psychic colleagues and I joke about putting our body armor on when we must go into the big-box stores! Personally, one thing I notice as my vibration continues to shift higher is that I cannot tolerate noise like I used to. By contrast, science has found that listening to music at 432 Hz helps shift our consciousness. Music tuned to 432 Hz helps align us with the heartbeat of the Universe.

Nature is a gift that helps us to unwrap our emotional blockages from the discord and hectic pace of our current world. Some people joke about tree huggers, and when they picture true tree huggers, 1970s hippies come to mind! But tree-hugging is beneficial to all of us. Science has proven that hugging and speaking kindly to trees, and even being in the vicinity of trees, positively affect our physical and mental well-being. Many spiritually minded people I know receive great benefits from walking barefoot on the earth. One of my husband Daniel's most profound spiritual experiences occurred when he lay beneath a tree and the tree began communicating with him. Connecting in this way to the raw grass, dirt, and trees can bring us a sense of safety, calmness, and serenity. As you raise your vibration, schedule time to unplug and commune with nature. Your aura will thank you!

PATIENCE AND COMPASSION

When you raise your vibration, your patience is improved, and you offer more compassion. Practicing more compassion for others is a wonderful way to shift your own vibration. Patience is certainly a virtue. When we are not rooted in the energy of patience, we tend to be anxious and nervous. These are lower-vibrational behaviors. When we learn to feel and express true patience, we remember that the opportunity to see the joy in every moment is ever before us, even if that happens while we are sitting in traffic or standing in a long line at the supermarket. (Especially then!) It is all about shifting the story we tell ourselves. In one of Edgar Cayce's channeled readings, he says, "When patience becomes an active principle in our lives, we rise above the boundaries of time and space. Our finite mind and our human side hold us in the dimensions of time and space, but we have access to our infinite mind. Our Christ-like side can and will lift us beyond time and space." For me, this is still one of my greatest challenges. I tend to feel justified and comfortable with being impatient. However, this is an area in which I am determined to pay attention and make progress every day! If this is also a challenge for you, please join me in setting the intention to remember the above words of Edgar Cayce.

INTUITION

When you raise your vibration and learn to stand in perfect alignment, your intuition is enhanced; therefore, you attract more people into your life who are living in truth. You have a greater chance of connecting with your soul tribe. You start to recognize that there are no coincidences, so when you experience synchronicities, you gratefully acknowledge them as signs from the Universe. I am adamant in my belief that everyone would do well to participate in a psychic or intuitive development program. A good intuitive development program teaches the difference between the expressions of Higher Self and ego. It describes the auric field, how to work best within that energy, and how to connect with your Angels and Spirit Guides. The Universe is an inconceivably magical, mystical place. One of the keys to a loving and productive life is to learn to tap into this magic. When we refine and strengthen our intuition, we more mindfully embrace obstacles and recognize their hidden opportunities. Teaching through my online school or at international events is one of my greatest joys, as I witness students embrace their intuition with confidence and grace.

This does not mean we do not allow our human emotions of disappointment, frustration, or sadness to express themselves. These emotions are essential parts of being a human being. It does mean that once we process emotions based on a perceived obstacle or a potential missed opportunity, we adjust and shift this energy into a higher spiritual perspective. The fourth density is a frequency in which we can begin to step out of the ego mind, embrace creativity, and allow occurrences we perceive as negative to shift into increasingly positive expressions.

What does this mean exactly? We consciously take a disappointing situation such as a job loss, a house falling through escrow, a relationship collapse, etc., and offer the situation up to the fourth dimension, allowing it to take on a different meaning and appearance. To do this, we must surrender and trust, centered and aligned with our Higher Selves. It may take a few hours, a few days, or even a few months for the new reality to present itself to us as an opportunity. When we are in the lower-density energy of disappointment, anger, frustration, or victimization, it is impossible to imagine that the situation could ever offer new and different possibilities.

When we learn to tap into this Divine Generosity, it is like always opening a gift! We simply must get out of the way and stop trying to paint the scenes to match our third-density ego wants, desires, and moods.

We each have a conduit straight to the Divine. When we learn to tap into and trust our intuitive guidance, inspiration and knowledge tend to flow effortlessly.

Relationship Changes

When someone does not vibrate on a level that matches your truth, you are more prepared to release them from your energy field. As your vibration shifts and changes, some of your friends and family may feel uneasy in your presence. Your joy, trust, and compassion for all tends to make them feel uncomfortable within themselves. Sometimes long-term friends, lovers, and spouses suddenly disappear for no reason. They may not even be able to explain it to themselves. It is important to remember that when people leave our lives, this creates more space and energy for those of like minds to take their place. As your vibration rises, it is as if you are sending a beam of light or radio signal to those who can recognize this radiance. Strive to be that beacon of illumination, and you will open doors to relationships you never dreamed possible.

This book is about going beyond the Law of Attraction. This chapter focuses on energy, vibration, and frequency. Once we understand the concepts of consciousness expansion, awakening to the truth of the Universe and weaving in the other Spiritual Laws, we are in proper alignment to practice manifestation magic.

Let us explore the shift in energy from the traditional teachings of the Law of Attraction to the more expansive approach of manifesting from a higher and deeper perspective.

Old Paradigm: Matt decides to manifest using the original teachings from *The Secret*. Matt declares, "Universe, I am the happy owner of a beautiful new Ferrari!" Matt is certain that a Ferrari is the car for him! Matt does not consider any soul contracts or infinite knowledge provided by his Spirit Team.

New Paradigm: Matt has finished reading *Manifesting Your Magic in the 5D*. In addition, he has spent time studying spirituality and the deeper meanings of the Universe while learning to tap into his intuition. He decides to employ manifestation magic using the techniques in this book.

So instead, Matt is inspired to say, "Universe, I would love a new car, and I trust the Universe to deliver it to me with the greatest of ease and in the highest and best way." Matt understands that in previous lives, he had amassed great wealth and had chosen to be quite greedy. In this lifetime, too, he has acquired financial abundance; however, he now chooses to share his wealth by taking care of animals and feeding the homeless. Matt's Spirit Team knows that a Ferrari is not the best option for carrying food to people and animals, nor is it the best vehicle for transporting animals who need help.

In the aura of Matt's trust and surrender, someone tells him about an almost new, beautiful SUV that just happens to be in his price range of comfort. As Matt drives home in his nearly new luxury SUV, he marvels and revels in gratitude about how amazing manifestation magic is. Some would argue that he failed at manifesting a Ferrari. Matt, by understanding the concepts in this book, would tell you that his role was to co-create something much better.

MANIFESTING IN THE QUANTUM

Now that we are excited about the positive changes that happen when we raise our vibrational frequency, let's explore simple ways to successfully manifest. To do this, we need to shift our awareness to the quantum level. The quantum field is a realm of infinite possibilities, where everything is interconnected, and potential realities exist simultaneously.

Before we dive into the steps, it is important for me to share some new insights from my Spirit Team about manifesting and navigating our lives.

In the old paradigm, our Spirit Guides provided us with guidance and strong suggestions if we were open to asking for and listening to their advice. However, the new paradigm shift involves a co-creative relationship with our Spirit Guides.

What does co-creation mean? Recently, my guides channeled added information to me indicating that starting in 2024, with the thinning of the veils, those of us who have been on our spiritual paths for some time will experience a different relationship with our Guides. They expressed a desire for dialogue, not just to offer suggestions. By embracing this new dynamic in our relationship, we are learning about empowerment and sovereignty.

A new channeling was then downloaded to me with instructions for making decisions. They guided us to take out a journal or blank sheet of paper and write down at least two or three potential timelines we are considering. If you are not familiar with the term "timeline," it simply refers to different options for how our lives might unfold.

To illustrate this concept, let us consider a decision Jane is facing. Jane is trying to decide whether to relocate to California or move to Portugal.

First, she will take out her journal or companion workbook and dedicate one page to detailing the timeline of moving to California. She will use this space to explore the pros and cons, engaging her imagination and creativity through inspirational writing.

Next, Jane will turn to another page in her journal to outline the timeline for moving to Portugal. She will document the pros and cons, envisioning the type of housing she might find, the friends she could meet, and the new foods and experiences she might encounter.

By writing out these details, Jane can vividly explore each option and start to lay the groundwork for her Spirit Guides to work with, aligning the possibilities with her soul's blueprint. This is step #1 in the process of quantum manifesting.

Step #2: To quiet our minds and calm the ego, listening to hertz frequency music can be beneficial. I prefer 741, 852, or 963 Hz. Try each one to see which resonates best with you. You might also experiment with different frequencies and observe how the changes affect your results.

Step #3: Once you are in a relaxed theta state, begin to engage in a dialogue with your Spirit Guides, seeking their input to help you make this decision. Set the intention to remain open and receptive to the signs and guidance they provide.

Step #4: Trust and surrender to the signs and synchronicities that begin to appear. Release the need to control the outcome and trust that the Universe has your back, guiding you according to your soul's blueprint.

Step #5: Express daily gratitude through mantras for the new paths and timelines that flow to you with ease.

INVITATION TO EXPLORE

Take some time to reflect on ways to shift your awareness to the true beauty of manifestation magic. Delve into some areas in your life where you can employ these concepts while releasing any remaining "in the box" constraints from the old Law of Attraction paradigm.

CHAPTER 8

COLLECTIVE WISDOM

What is collective wisdom? According to Wikipedia, collective wisdom is shared knowledge arrived at by individuals and groups, used to solve problems and conflicts of *all humanity*. Drawing from the reservoir of Universal Truth, the point of collective wisdom is to make life easier/more enjoyable through understanding human behavior. Wisdom is not used for "self" to bring in wealth, abundance, soulmate love, or fame. Wisdom is understood and acted upon for the benefit of all humanity! How beautiful is this? Imagine for a moment that every person on Mother Earth understood and practiced collective wisdom.

Some of you may wonder if it is wrong or ineffectual for you to continue praying, using mantras, and practicing positive visualizations. Of course, it is not wrong! These practices go hand in hand with the bringing in of collective wisdom. There is nothing wrong with wishing for abundance, true love, a fulfilling career path, and financial success. However, it is important to understand that now that the Phoenix Days are upon us, our current financial system will be changing from what it is now. Our current system is unsustainable. I predict that more people will begin bartering as focus shifts to smaller communities working together for the greater good of everyone in that community. You can already see this dynamic at work with the rise of community co-ops and local farmers markets. Community-based trade provides a beautiful opportunity for us to get back to the basics of connecting on a deeper level. The ripple effect of these minor changes will be far-reaching.

The balance of karma is always in play. Too many people bought into The Law of Attraction and The Secret solely out of greed and for personal gain without considering the many other truths that go along with them. We must each have faith that we can handle any situations or drawbacks that appear before us. This is part of our spiritual path and our personal soul growth, which also contributes to the soul growth of all. Practicing this brings us closer to the unconditional loving energy of our God Force.

The key to your own spiritual practice is coming to a knowing and an understanding of what your life purpose is during this current incarnation. Maybe your soul needed to experience being homeless or losing your wealth. Or maybe you needed to experience grief for a loved one who has crossed over? Like me, maybe you needed the experience of a lifetime in which you did not have the gift of being a biological parent. For me too was the gut-wrenching grief of losing my mom, who was also my mentor and best friend.

One vital area that ego driven law of attraction leaves out is the Universal Truth that as each of us advances further toward enlightenment and a vibrational energetic level closer to the God Source, our challenges sometimes become greater. Maybe one individual has chosen a life of fame and wealth. And let us say that during this chosen life of fame and wealth, the soul has other areas of work to attend to. And for some, their life purpose is holding space and the energy of proper frequency for others.

As I have previously explained, everything in our Universe consists of energy and vibrational frequencies that can be measured. Once we learn to tap into this Universal Intelligence, we become part of what I like to refer to as Limitless Information for Everyone, or L.I.F.E. One of the "clair" words used to describe the ability of certain kinds of psychics is Claircognizance. Claircognizance is a clear knowing without understanding *how* you know the information. My Spirit Team has taught me that Claircognizance is the ability to tap into the Collective Consciousness (Collective Intelligence). This is the realm of shared knowledge. My Team has shown it to me as being like a databank or hard drive of information stored in the ethers. However, it is not stored in the ethers; they have shown it to me this way so that my third-dimensional human brain can try to conceptualize this information. When you stop and think about it, this makes perfect sense! When someone claircognizantly *knows* information about a subject yet has not *consciously* learned it in this lifetime, the Collective Intelligence *would* be the "place" this information comes from! How exciting is this concept my Spirit Team has shown me? This is another reason to study and learn psychic development with a qualified instructor. The more you learn to harness your psychic gifts, the easier it will be for you to tap into Collective Intelligence. How awesome to have a wealth of knowledge at your fingertips anytime you need access! Channeling is yet another way that information not previously known can come through an individual. The channel connects to a higher being or consciousness and receives information that he or she had no way of knowing before the channeling session.

I have channeled an entity called Ashtar, of the Ashtar Command. The first time I met Ashtar, he came to me in the middle of the night and introduced himself. I had never heard of him before that evening. He telepathically said, "I am Ashtar of the Ashtar Command, and I would like to work with you." I was so startled that I jumped out of bed and googled Ashtar Command. There it was as plain as day from others who had channeled him! People get a kick out of the fact that psychics and mediums still get awed! If you have read my first book, *Mississippi Medium: My Journey from Southern Baptist to Talking to the Dead*, you may recall some of my out-of-this-world experiences. Yet, I still have those jaw-dropping moments of *wow, did this really just happen*?! I cannot imagine living a so-called normal mundane life when we have such magic at our fingertips to uncover every day!

Ashtar is part of a consciousness called The Collective, that has volunteered to help those of us residing in the third dimension to awaken and ascend. Ashtar and his Galactic Team are also assisting us in breaking free from the matrix. Human beings have found themselves embedded in a control dynamic limited further by the Internet and social media. These higher-dimensional beings are channeling information through me and others to help us break these barriers and free ourselves from the matrix of domination. Primarily in recent history, the matrix of domination is mainly experienced by women and African Americans. When Ashtar channeled this term to me, the energy surrounding it was shown to be that of domination by those individuals vibrating at such a low frequency that we consider them evil. Their agenda is control through manipulation. Manipulation of our money supply, media, and pitting us against each other. Their maneuver of encouraging us to "choose sides" causes further division and alienation. And the further separated we think we are, the further we are from awareness of our true state of unity. Until most humans can see that they are voluntarily participating in this system, true ascension of the collective cannot reach the fifth dimension. Part of this lesson lies in transcending this pattern and breaking free of the limiting beliefs that make up this reality.

How can we transcend these thought and belief patterns? There are many ways to accomplish this. One way is by tuning into the wisdom of your heart. I believe that our hearts harbor greater Universal Intelligence than our brains do. And scientific research supports this. Heart Math has been one of the premier research institutions studying the heart and brain connection. Rollin McCraty, Ph.D., one of Heart Math's founders, said, "The biggest hidden source of stress on the planet is the disorganization of heart/mind, causing lack of resonance. Lack of alignment eats the life force and happiness out of humanity." McCraty also claims that the heart has access to information outside the boundaries of time and space.

How do we learn to listen to the intelligence or intuition of the heart? By going within. By unplugging from the mass media which continually feeds us traumas and lower-vibrational words and images. Meditating, communing with nature, and learning to tune into our hearts. One thing I teach my psychic and mediumship students is always to make sure they are delivering messages to their clients from their heart chakra, always making sure the unique messages to themselves and others are from their heart space. The limiting human ego stemming from the brain's knowledge base is largely bypassed.

Grasping the exciting fact that we are co-creators of our Universe is another way to transcend our limiting and separative beliefs. What do I mean by co-creators? Our Creator has given us free will. If we can break the limiting mindset that fate and destiny are set in stone and the details of our lives have already been molded, true freedom can occur. Imagine a world where we can wake up each day and write a new life script!

That world is here right in front of us! This is the gloriously liberating truth of what it means to co-create our reality.

A stunning visualization my Spirit Team has shown me is of starting each day in quiet contemplation, allowing guidance to come in, not only from our personal Spirit Team and Guides but also from the Collective Wisdom. The more we tap into this collective, the more freedom we will feel to co-create without boundaries. We humans are only using a tiny portion of our potential.

Some of you may feel I contradict myself with the information in chapter 5 regarding soul contracts. I believe that we do agree to certain soul contracts before we incarnate. This is our soul's way of experiencing opportunities for growth and evolution. Yet, with free will, we can set in motion the way our life is experienced as it unfolds. The difference is this: In the past, we have been taught that we can manifest anything our hearts desire. The *new* key is this: Before we set the intention of our manifestation, our consciousness needs to shift. If we are manifesting from our 3D perspective, our human ego will certainly get in the way. However, if we learn to release our human control and manifest from a higher vibration, this helps us release the limitations our human brain automatically puts on us.

When we are in a quiet space of meditation, we are already tapping into a higher-vibrational frequency. This is the place for manifestation magic to occur!

Another asset we humans have at our disposal is the Star Children who have incarnated. Star Children are human children born to help us heal our planet and ascend to higher vibrations. Many books have been written about Star Children; you may even be a Star Child yourself. Some common names for such children are indigo, crystal, rainbow, and diamond. Star Children either arrive as a soul from a higher-vibrational frequency or a planet that vibrates at a higher frequency than our own. They are born already knowing we are all connected. Star

Children have a special affinity for animals, plants, and nature. They tend to be quite sensitive and are often misunderstood.

Lee Carroll who channels Kryon first channeled information about Star Children in the 1970s. Since then, there has been much more information given regarding these souls. Many people believe that these children are a human/alien hybrid. It is my personal belief that the vast majority of highly psychic individuals have had contact with aliens and so-called UFOs. I realize that for many people, this concept may seem far-fetched. As I have always said, I must share my firsthand experiences from a place of honesty and truth. And my truth is that I am a Star Seed who has experienced visitation from aliens or extra-terrestrials my entire life. Therefore, the information channeled by Lee Carroll and others has a huge resonance of truth for me.

There are several ways you can differentiate the various breeds of Star Seeds. The difference can be seen by certain gifted psychics in the color of the aura. Most Indigo children are predominantly blue in their auric field. Crystal Children have a clearer or quartz-colored aura, and Rainbow Children have an aura consisting of a prism of several colors at one time. They also have vastly different and distinct personalities.

Several years ago, sometime around 2014, in meditation with the amazing spiritual teacher Lucy Finch of Altered Elements in Naples, Florida, I experienced a profound revelation. I was told that one of my soul contracts was to channel and author a book about the new children arriving. My human ego argued with my Spirit Team that I had not even had biological children in this lifetime, and how was I supposed to channel a book about children? I was told: This is part of your mission, and as an Indigo Star Seed yourself, you have the tools to compre-hend and dissect the information channeled to you. During that meditation, I was told that the new children arriving would be named The Children of the Golden Ray and would be seen by those who can see auras as having a golden aura. I asked if any of these children had incarnated, and I was told no. Since that time, I have been shown that the Golden Ray Children began incarnating in 2017. They are arriving from the twelfth dimension of consciousness. I am over the moon excited to channel the information on these children and write a book about them!

I have already had the pleasure of connecting with several parents of Golden Ray Children. The first one was when I was doing a reading for a couple in Asheville, North Carolina, and they asked me to tune into their young daughter and provide any information I could to help them parent her. As I tuned into her frequency, I immediately recognized the golden aura I had been shown several years ago. The purity of her auric field was awe-inspiring. As tears streamed down my face, I told this couple they were parents to a daughter from a new breed of Star Children called The Golden Rays. They were both quite emotional yet felt the sincerity of validation as they had always known she was quite different. The second one was a child still in utero. As I was channeling information from one of my client's spirit guides, I was told that the child she was close to birthing into the world was a Golden Ray Child. I sat in awe as I connected with this divine being. My client admitted that she had experienced a deep knowing that this child was different. I explained how important it was for her as this gifted child's mother to ensure she aligned her intuition and frequency, so she was equipped to parent this child in the highest good for all. This Golden Ray Mom registered for mine and Duann's Intuitive Development Classes immediately.

Making the shift from a third-dimensional consciousness to a fifth-dimensional consciousness requires knowledge of certain steps. I enjoy seeing this as a bridge to another level of awareness. As we progress through our lives and begin to expand our individual awareness to include greater possibilities never imagined, we begin to receive glimpses of this cosmic bridge. As we do our own inner work, all the while healing and growing, we draw closer to this bridge e so that we not only see it, but also grasp certain understandings about it. Part of this knowing is that once we decide to step onto this bridge and begin walking, we can never turn back. Once you step into the awe-inspiring magical energy of the bridge, you do not *want* to go back! You understand that the old world you left behind on the other side of that bridge is mundane and limiting. The energy of the old world feels confining and contracted. By contrast, the fifth dimension holds an expansive frequency. Simply walking on the bridge brings you an excitement you never dreamed possible. Effortlessly and instantly, you feel the oneness of the fifth dimension. Standing on this cosmic bridge, you witness and participate in the miracles unfolding in the beauty surrounding you.

Part of the challenge of these times is navigating the world from the third dimension to the fifth. Many of us have tried to keep one foot on either side of this bridge for many years. Those who have experienced this understand it is not the easiest of tasks! And the longer you choose to linger on the fifth-dimensional side of the bridge, the more complicated it becomes to reside at all on the 3D side. It becomes almost impossible. It is important to acknowledge the fact that your physical body cannot remain in the old energy, but also important not to judge those who have chosen to stay on the 3D side. We each have free will and can make these choices. I invite those who have yet to experience this awesome energy to begin their journey to the bridge. I promise you: Your life will be forever enriched.

In 2009, my friend and colleague Sally Rice and I both received the same message from our Spirit Team. We were told that there would come a time in the future when there would be no more gray areas. At that time, souls would make a conscious choice of where they would reside. Which side of the bridge if you will. That time is now. Now that we have entered the new decade of the 2020s, a choice must be made. As our Mother Earth raises her vibrational frequency, it is becoming increasingly difficult for those who have chosen to remain in the unity energy of the fifth dimension to be in the energy of those who have consciously chosen to remain in the ego-dense energy of the divisive third dimension.

In closing this chapter, I would like to present this concept in a nice tidy package with a pretty bow on top! We are all interconnected by an etheric silver cord leading to the Infinite Source of all, our Creator God force. The essence of our Creator is true unconditional love for all, and the higher we can raise our vibrational frequency, the greater our experience of a love without condition or limitation. Given that we are truly interconnected—woven together like threads in a design of ever-changing fabric—I think it reasonable to assume that as we raise our vibration and set the intention to help raise the vibration of others from a place of love and oneness, we all benefit.

Previous books on manifesting have done an outstanding job of introducing the concept of the Law of Attraction. Yet, in some instances, readers distorted the teachings to accommodate an extreme of greed, thereby stepping further into the energy of "me, myself, and I." In the fourteen years since this best-selling book was published, humanity has raised its collective vibrational frequency. It is now time to shift our mindset and consciousness to an energy of "we." The *Secret of the Secret* is so simple, yet one must achieve a certain level of awareness and energy vibration to comprehend how to set the wheels in motion truly. If you are reading this book, it is more than likely this shift has already occurred in your conscious awareness.

We are living in extraordinary times. It is a beautiful honor to have incarnated during these momentous shifts in evolution and consciousness. Each day, we are offered the gift of co-creating an exciting, magnificent Universe where all benefit in some way. This is needed to bring in the Age of Peace and Enlightenment.

INVITATION TO EXPLORE

I urge you to create an individual practice of beginning each day in quiet contemplation. Set the intention that you are now the co-creator of your reality and your world, with no boundaries or limitations.

As you become more adept at co-creating your Universe, you will begin to notice that as long as you have applied the other Spiritual Laws in this book and you embrace your connection with all others, your individual wants and needs will begin to dovetail with those of all of humanity. And within this shift, you will begin to tap into limitless abundance for all. What does this mean? It simply means that the mentality of lack and poverty will gradually fade away, and your desires for an abundant life for yourself will emerge from your co-creating a Universe wherein *everyone* is divinely blessed. Can you *feel* the difference in manifesting in this way versus sitting in silence, visualizing, and affirming for all you are worth that snazzy Ferrari and cocktails on the deck of *your* mansion?

Journal about your experiences and watch the magic unfold!

CHAPTER 9

PAINTING YOUR MASTERPIECE

"Sometimes when we gaze at the canvas of our life, our painting may not appear flawless. Yet with each exquisite stroke, a beautiful masterpiece of divine perfection begins to emerge."

In this closing chapter, I will weave together nine practical steps to achieve the best version of your masterpiece. Most of us will not realize enlightenment during this lifetime; however, the goal is to show up each day and be the best version of ourselves that we can be. If we remember that every moment of every day, we have choices, making God-informed choices will be uppermost in our mind. Our thoughts are choices. We can choose positive ones, or we can choose to engage in stinkin' thinkin.' The choice is ours. With awakening comes the realization that we are all beautiful works in progress. And the more we know who we are on a soul level, the more we can be honest with ourselves.

Along with the raw splendor of honesty comes the opportunity for forgiveness, forgiveness of ourselves and others. Forgiveness is not about excuses, nor is it about holding on to stagnant energy from sorrows of the past. It pains me when I have clients who cannot forgive someone from their past and move forward into the present. They have recorded a mini movie in their mind about how much they have been hurt and wronged, and they hit replay almost daily. Be honest and ask yourself if you have one of these recordings in your psyche that you will gladly play for anyone listening. Receiving compassion from another person for the pains you have endured provides but a momentary lift to the energy field. Yet when the recording is over and the other person moves forward with their own life, we are forced to accept the energy of where this leaves us.

We each have the choice to edit or scrap our mini movies! Proudly put on your writer's cap and begin articulating your life's new script. Remind yourself to step into fifth-dimensional energy prior to picking up the pen or striking the keys. Release limitations as you create. And as you sit in the director's chair, invite your Spirit Guides to join you in navigating the exciting plot twists and turns along the way. Remember that your Guides are holding the original script that you agreed to prior to incarnating. The inspiring thing is this. With our God-given free will, we can meet with our Spirit Team and co-create fresh and innovative scenarios anytime we choose!

These are the nine steps that have helped me create my masterpiece. As you adopt these steps, you will find it easier to create your own awe-inspiring canvas.

1. **Remove the Ego**—What is the definition of ego? According to Merriam-Webster, ego is the self, especially as contrasted with another self or the world. Ego is the Latin word for "I." As we strive to embrace the vibration of the fifth dimension,

we must remember that the new frequency is about the "we" and not the "I." Everything in life is about balance and moderation. I am not suggesting that we should not have healthy self-esteem and sense of self-worth. However, ego keeps us in a place of separation and not unity. As Eckhart Tolle writes in *A New Earth*, "Give up defining yourself—to yourself or to others... Whenever you interact with people, do not be there primarily as a function or a role, but as the field of conscious Presence. You can only lose something that you have, but you cannot lose something that you are." This is what I am referring to when I recommend that you lose the more selfish aspects of ego. When we truly grasp we are souls having an experience in a human body, the ego becomes much less of a factor. Our ego is involved in judgment and our rational, critical thinking processes. Prioritizing our ego prevents us from transcending old, outdated thought processes. The sweet spot is getting to know the awareness behind the physical and material aspects of who we are and the role we play in this world. And by leaving the ego behind, we discover our true identity.

2. **Calm the Mind**—It is impossible to remain open, balanced, properly connected to Source Energy without devoting time to quiet the mind. This idea seems so simple, yet lack of time is one of the most common excuses I hear from my clients and others. *I cannot quiet my mind,* some say. *My mind never stops working,* is the mantra of others. My response is this:" Then you need meditation even more!" Everyone should also be practicing some form of yoga. Yoga provides a space for retreat from our busy daily lives. When we show up and step onto our mat, we begin to train our minds to be present and in the moment. This is referred to as mindfulness. Mindfulness is learning to focus attention on what you are experiencing in the present moment

without judging yourself. Practicing yoga has been shown to increase mindfulness not only while we are in the class, but in every aspect of our lives. When we are living in the now, in the present moment, we are more easily able to let go of the past and stop fretting about the future.

3. **Practice Detachment**—We have become a society that places terrific value on material possessions. Many people define who they are based on the size of their house, or how many homes they own, the brand of their watches, the designer label on their clothes, etc. I am not suggesting we should not desire nice things or luxurious items. Luxury is...well... luxurious! What I am referring to is the energy behind the possessions. I invite you to examine the why around your possessions and be honest with yourself about whether you desire something because it provides you with some level of comfort or joy, or whether you hold on to it to make a *statement* to other people. For example, there was a time in my life when I had a goal to own a Rolex. At the place I was in my life, this was one way I put a price tag on my level of success. The Law of Attraction worked for me, and I purchased a watch that cost me over $5,000. Looking back and being candidly honest with myself, I can see that wearing the watch made me *feel* more successful. Yet, in the grand scheme of things, the watch had nothing to do with my success! And then, as life often does in providing us growth opportunities, I found myself in a place where I needed to sell the watch to pay for necessities. At first, I was heartbroken. I told myself that I had worked so hard for that watch, and I would certainly miss wearing it. In my moments of despair and feeling sorry for myself, my energetic vibration was certainly lowered. Yet, through detachment from this material item, I was given an opportunity to honestly examine the *why* of the watch I had chosen. Did the watch tell

better time than my Timex or other watches had? No, it did not! When I sat honestly with myself, it became apparent that I wanted the watch so *others* would see and admire the level of my supposed success. At that time in my evolution, I valued what others thought of me more than who I knew myself to be. A similar story from my friend and colleague psychic medium Sally Rice brings a smile to my face. Sally had attained a great amount of material wealth throughout her life. One of her prized possessions was a Prada purse. During her spiritual evolution and consciousness expansion, her Spirit Guides softly suggested that she release the attachment to her Prada purse. Sally argued and pouted as we humans tend to, and said aloud, "But I love my Prada purse!" And then, she decided to conduct a little experiment with the Universe. Sally declared, "OK, Universe! I will drop off my Prada at a nonprofit, and I will release my attachment to this purse, but in return, I want some sort of acknowledgement that my deed has been noticed." Sally was attempting to practice her own version of the Law of Attraction while expanding her consciousness level. After dropping off her beloved Prada purse and stepping into the energy of complete detachment, she drove to a healthy grocery store to pick up a few items. As she walked inside, a nice young man approached her and said, "Hi, I have a gift for you." Sally, never one to turn down a sincere gift, followed him back out to the parking lot and he opened the back of his van. "My wife hand-sews beautiful purses, and my Spirit Guides just told me to give one of them to you." He continued, "I'm not sure why I'm supposed to gift you with one, but I have learned to listen to my Team, so please take the purse and enjoy it." Sally marveled at the magic that had just unfolded before her eyes and thanked the Universe for the proof she had requested. This event still makes me tear up. We truly do live in a magical place of abundance. I invite you to examine some of the material possessions you have acquired. Be honest with yourself. Do you have these possessions because they bring you joy or comfort, or do you have them to impress others? Again, there is absolutely nothing wrong with luxury and comfort! Luxuries are among the gifts showered upon us by this amazing planet we call home. The lesson lies in detaching from the place of ego.

4. **Spiritual Mentors and Teachers**—I would not be where I am today without the lessons learned from my spiritual teachers and mentors. It saddens me when people say, "I don't need classes or knowledge from others, because I was born with my wisdom and gifts." This is pure ego. We ALL have something to learn from others who have either experienced more life lessons or who have studied with others to share the knowledge they received. Semi-jokingly I say to my students, "With certain spiritual teachers, you learn how you *don't* want to be or how you *don't* want to do things!" Yet, you still learned something. This does not mean that you place all your questions and answers to life in someone else's hands. It simply means that you are receptive to the knowledge and insights of others, learning from them while honoring your guidance. You take what resonates with you from the wisdom of each teacher and kindly leave the rest behind. We should never stop learning and growing! I crave to learn from others who have more life experience than I do. This does not lessen my value as a spiritual teacher. In fact, it strengthens it. I still laugh when I recall something one of my spiritual teachers, John Holland, shared with our class. By making a joke, John showed his reverence and respect for one of his teachers, James Van Praagh. John chuckled as he told us students, "As I climb the ladder of my success, I am always looking up at the

behind of James Van Praagh." He goes on to say, "And I am OK with that! What an honor to be staring up at James's behind as I climb higher myself! James will always be a few rungs above me because he has had more experience in the world of mediumship." Show reverence and respect for your spiritual teachers. No matter how many years I have been serving the Spirit World, I have never lost respect for the teachers I have had along the way. It does not mean that I give my power away to them. It simply means I honor what they taught me and how they assisted me along my soul's path. You would do well to find a spiritual teacher whom you feel drawn to; then watch your life burst into colors and shapes you could never have imagined.

5. **Learn Vibrational Frequency**—Living a human experience gives us vast opportunities to learn from our mistakes. With practice and dedication, we can learn to keep our thoughts pure, our words uplifting, and our actions wholesome. Strive to be an inspiration to others. I urge you to always be on the lookout to help one another with this, as practice makes perfect. If you hear a friend or loved one speaking words that put themselves or another down, even jokingly, tell them to cancel-clear their words and speak them over again positively. Get in the habit of bearing witness to your own words and the energy behind them. Have fun with this. Leave little love notes around the house that you will find with sayings such as "I am abundant," "I am healthy," "I am kind," "I am an inspiration to others," etc. Consider how your energy level will automatically shift when you encounter these uplifting words. Another fun thing we can do to help shift other people's energy is to offer them kind words, such as genuine compliments and encouragement. Make a pact with yourself that you will choose at least one stranger a day whom you will compliment or cheer in some

way. You can compliment what they are wearing or their beautiful eyes or smiles. Recently, I told a woman that she had a beautiful aura, and her grateful smile lit up the room. When we compliment someone, we in turn get an energy boost. Win-win and joy-joy for everyone!

6. **Engage in Life**—As discussed in chapter four, we cannot manifest our heart's desires without understanding the Spiritual Law of Action. When we actively participate in our lives and take the necessary steps in the direction of something we desire, momentum is created, which in turn helps activate the Law of Vibration and brings more success to the Law of Attraction. For example, it takes more than a desire for someone to fulfill their ambition to be the greatest athlete of all time. Along with that desire comes dedication and actually putting the steps into motion to reach the desired result. First, the right coach or mentor must be located. After the trainer is found, certain hours of each day must be spent on training. The Law of Attraction will not work if the athlete simply sits there in lotus position, willing him or herself to be the greatest athlete of all time. I have told countless clients that the chance of their soulmate simply walking up to their front door one day and sweeping them off their feet is highly unlikely. We must take action to get involved in activities that bring us joy and excitement, actions that puts us in situations where we are likely to meet our soulmates. When we actively show up as excited participants in our lives, this sends the Universe an energy signature that we are doing our part to harness our hopes and dreams.

Remaining fluid and adaptable helps a great deal in engaging in life. For instance, if we choose to live in the same box without ever stepping outside of it or being open to new experiences, a stuck and stagnant energy ensues.

My recommendation is this: Do not simply climb outside your box. Make designs with your box. Mold it into various geometric shapes and see what excitement the Universe delivers to your doorstep then! And I promise you, if you are true to this task, the "box" the Universe delivers your gifts in will look like nothing you could have ever imagined! Always remember you are the co-creator of your Universe, so have fun with this.

7. **Release Your Fears**—Facing one's fears is not for the faint of heart. However, since we know that everything is energy and everything we think, feel, and do comprise energy, we must come to terms with our fears holding us back. Fear is a low-vibrational energy. Fear is a lack of trust. With his usual humor, Mark Twain said, "I have been through some terrible things in my life, some of which happened." When I feel myself slipping into the energy of fear, I ask myself, "What is the worst that can happen?" It is important not to sweep our fears under the proverbial rug, because fear is a legitimate human emotion. Yet if we can learn to shift our fears into courage and compassion, just imagine the sublime results we will witness. I simply adore this quote from Marianne Williamson: "Our deepest fear is not that we are inadequate. Our deepest fear is that we are powerful beyond measure. It is our light, not our darkness, that most frightens us. We ask ourselves, 'Who am I to be brilliant, gorgeous, talented, fabulous?' Actually, who are you not to be? You are a child of God." In order to manifest the divine masterpiece that you were meant to create, you must release your fears. This does not mean we scold ourselves for our fears. It means that we lovingly learn to turn our fears into courage. We simply cannot walk a spiritual path burdened by our fears. This is not something that happens overnight, however. There are legitimate fears that arise

while changing and evolving. Sometimes, things and people will leave our lives as we expand beyond their comfort zones. Honor the grief of the loss while bravely recognizing that someone leaving our lives creates space for others to step in. And congratulate yourself for the fears you have transcended on the liberating wings of courage.

8. **Trust and Surrender**—As discussed in chapter 4, the Spiritual Law of Faith plays a key role in manifesting our masterpieces. The word surrender sounds so sexy, sultry, and easy, yet it is one of the most challenging states for humans to realize. We feel powerful when we are in control. It gives us a false sense of comfort and security. Yet that's just it. Ultimately, is a *false* sense of protection. In my humble view of spiritual evolution, we must learn to trust not only ourselves, but also our Creator and Spirit Team. We must discern the difference between trusting ourselves when we are in perfect alignment with our Higher Selves and trusting ourselves when we behave foolishly, without regard for ourselves and others.

9. **Unconditional Love and Oneness**—If I needed to choose just one word to represent the energy of the fifth dimension, it would certainly be oneness. It is impossible to experience oneness in the third dimension. Oneness extends beyond the five senses, beyond the ordinary reality. Have you ever felt pure bliss, and the ecstasy was so sublime that you had a moment of feeling at one with All That Is, and more? These are fleeting glimpses of what awaits us in the higher dimensions. My Guides have shown me that as we move into 2020 and beyond, our attention needs to be focused on loving ourselves first. If we cannot genuinely love ourselves   without conditions, it is not possible for us to genuinely love another. And by fully loving every aspect of

ourselves, we are reminded that we are indeed One. I invite you to practice standing in front of the mirror each morning and gazing deeply into your eyes to the depths of your soul, saying, "I love you." This is powerful medicine, my friends.

It has been my honor to accompany you on this journey with me. I sincerely hope you have received additional inspiration by raising the curtain on previously private scenes of my heartbreak and grief and making my best effort to share the discoveries I have made along the way. "Powerful beyond measure," you are now equipped to paint your own divine masterpiece in ways that excite and delight you.

Finally, I thank Rhonda Byrne for introducing us to *The Secret* eighteen years ago. The concepts in her best-selling book went a long way toward waking people up to their unlimited worthiness and infinite potential. My hope is that by reading my book, you have received some profound and enlightening secrets that will further assist you on your life's amazing journey.

The Light in me sees and honors the Light in each of you. Namaste.

EPILOGUE

To Mandy's delight, the small town of Fairhope, Alabama, was majestically beautiful. And the people were so friendly and welcoming. *I guess there is truth to what people say about Southern hospitality*, Mandy found herself thinking. Fairhope was close enough to her job in Mobile to make her commute effortless. She and Teddy had settled into a small cottage within walking distance of the cute downtown area. While she liked her job and the people who worked there, Mandy knew in her heart of hearts that there was more she wanted to accomplish in her life.

Mandy spent her free time enjoying yoga and meditation, which had helped her reach a deeper place of contemplation. She was reading books on spirituality and ascension which were really helping her understand the deeper meanings of life and the Universe. However, she was still flustered and frustrated over her perceived manifestation failures over the past year. Nevertheless, Mandy knew how important staying positive and paying attention to her thoughts and emotions was. As she woke to the dawn of each new day, she reminded herself to practice gratitude for her courage and how far she had come. She felt peaceful and more in alignment than she ever had before. Mandy yearned for companionship, yet she had detached herself from putting constraints on what this actually looked like or how it would manifest for her. And she certainly recognized that she had been settling and trying to fit a square peg into a round hole in her years spent with John. Over time, she had forgiven him and even performed a healing cord-cutting ceremony at an event she had attended the month prior. She was finally at peace with his infidelity and the choices he had made, recognizing that negative thoughts of him took up precious real estate in the recesses of her mind.

One beautiful June day, Mandy decided to walk to her favorite coffee shop. She had grown to love and adore the small town of Fairhope and finally felt at home living there. There were times, however, in her daydreams that the Florida beaches would seem to call out her name, their waves whispering sweet nothings in her ear. And when she really allowed herself to reflect on what she would want to be remembered for, the animals and their welfare always came to mind. But for now, she considered herself happy and content at this juncture in her life.

"Your regular caramel latte with coconut milk, Mandy?" Paige smiled as Mandy entered the café. "Sounds heavenly," Mandy said as she settled into a comfy chair by the large bay window. They exchanged pleasantries and Paige told Mandy another hilarious story about her new rescue dog, Lucky. As Mandy sipped her latte, she noticed a handsome man walk into the shop. As their eyes met, she felt—although she knew it was perhaps a corny allusion—that her world had stopped turning. After he grabbed a coffee, he walked over to Mandy and introduced himself. "Hi, I'm Alex," he smiled, holding out his hand in greeting. Mandy tried to gather her composure as she introduced herself but felt as if she would disappear into the depths of his green eyes and be unable to come back out! "Do you mind if I join you? I'm just here visiting for a few days. I live in Pensacola, where I run an animal rescue nonprofit, and I needed a break!" He continued, "As you can imagine, it's a lot of work, but a passion that I care a great deal about."

Mandy noted that the sensation she was experiencing reminded her of the strange feeling she had felt in Ms. Thelma's presence. There was a calm yet electric sensation in the pit of her stomach. Two hours passed as Mandy and Alex effortlessly chatted as if they had known each other forever. In truth, they both felt they had been reunited with someone who was monumental in their lives. Alex invited Mandy to dinner that night, and over dessert she recounted her lifelong dream of rescuing animals. Mandy felt a sense of safety with Alex that she had never felt before. Every time she gazed into his kind eyes, she sensed that he knew her to the depths of her soul. They spent every moment together over the next few days and, as Alex prepared his return to Florida, he admitted to Mandy that he had never honestly believed in love at first sight until now. He explained that he was secure in where he was in his life and had not really dated since his divorce several years back, but after meeting her, he could not imagine a life without her in it. Mandy told Alex she felt the same way.

As fate would have it, their commute to see each other was only a one-hour drive. They continued dating and getting to know each other over the next eight months and on Valentine's Day, Alex got down on his knee and proposed. Later that night, Mandy was reminded that the proposal was exactly as she had envisioned a couple of years back. The only difference was the person down on one knee. *Wow, this is interesting*! Mandy reflected. *Maybe the Law of Attraction does work*. However, there were other factors at play, not yet known. Alex and Mandy planned a June wedding on the shores of Fairhope, Alabama, 12 months to the day from when they had met. Mandy was thrilled when she found the perfect wedding dress, identical to the one she had cut out of a magazine when she was still living in Michigan. When Alex took Mandy's hand in his to proudly say his vows, tears were streaming down both of their faces.

Mandy's coworkers were sad to see her leave, but over-the-moon happy at the love she had found. Three months after moving to Florida and going to work with Alex at his animal rescue foundation, Mandy received yet another surprise. Alex came home filled with childlike excitement as he told her to get in the car with him. "We are going on a little adventure!" Alex said, his eyes dancing with enthusiasm. As they pulled up to the house Alex had discovered for them, Mandy shook her head in disbelief. The house looked exactly like the one she had cut out from the magazine while living in Michigan. *How could this be?* she wondered. Alex twirled Mandy around as she kissed him all over his face. "I love it," she declared.

They settled in and made the house their home. Mandy's favorite part of the house was the large fenced-in yard, which gave their many rescue dogs plenty of room to play. Of course, the dogs lived inside with them as part of their family, but Shanti, their massive Lab and shepherd mix, adored running as fast as she could around the expansive yard, chasing the less than thrilled border collie.

A few months later, Mandy's friend Denise mailed her a copy of a book she had just read and loved. Mandy sat down and devoured the pages of *Manifesting Your Magic in the 5D*, in a few short days. Her mind was reeling as the words on each page finally answered her questions about why she had previously been unsuccessful at using the Law of Attraction to manifest. Mandy smiled as she realized she had successfully manifested everything she had wanted. It just took various twists and turns and had different timing than what she had in mind. The fact that she was living on the beaches of Florida with her soulmate while helping him run an animal rescue still sent shockwaves of delight down her spine. "What are the odds?" Mandy asked Teddy, curled up by her side. Teddy gifted her with a sly gaze and smile, as he absolutely adored Alex. *All Mom had to do was ask me all those years ago and I would have told her how it was*, Teddy surmised in his innate kitty wisdom.

Later that night over dinner, Mandy shared with Alex all she had read in the book Denise had sent her. Alex commented, "I guess it would make sense that we have other Spiritual Laws at our fingertips to use along with the Law of Attraction. And one is not any more important than the others." Mandy smiled as she reflected on how she had put the Law of Faith in place when she trusted and surrendered and moved to Alabama. "I could have used my free will and chosen to ignore the signs and synchronicities and forced a move to Florida," she shared with her husband, "but it would not have been Pensacola, and I would probably not have met you."

As Mandy lay in bed holding Alex's hand that night, she marveled at how amazing life can be if we learn to get out of our way. An inspiring vision wafted through her mind of herself teaching and leading workshops, coaching others in the use of all the Spiritual Laws to paint the masterpiece of their lives. *I will put the Law of Action into play and research the best places to lead the workshops, watching for signs and synchronicities to light my way.* She then offered up her prayers of gratitude, reminding herself of the words Ms. Thelma had said to her all those years ago about the riches of the Universe falling at her feet. "This magical, mystical Universe has certainly delivered riches in ways I never dreamt possible," Mandy whispered as she closed her eyes, excited for the dreams to come.

ABOUT THE AUTHOR

Jill M. Jackson is an internationally celebrated **Psychic Medium, Spiritual Teacher**, and published **Author**. She is the recipient of the prestigious Psychic of the Year award two years in a row from *Best American Psychics*, as well as its 2014 Social Activism Award for her volunteer work with animals.

One of her great passions is serving as a **Spiritual Teacher** and helping others ignite, refine, and hone their intuition! Seeing her students undergo this magical transformation is a joy to Jill's soul, and their testimony speaks to her passion and brilliance as a mentor. Consider allowing Jill to help you navigate your way! Visit www.JillMJackson.com.

Jill's authorial debut, *Mississippi Medium: My Journey from Southern Baptist to Talking to the Dead,* is a must-read for anyone on the path of awakening. It continues to receive 5-star reviews.

Jill's upcoming book, *Children of the New Earth,* introduces the groundbreaking concept of a new "breed" of children who began incarnating in 2015. These New Earth children arrive on the 12th ray of consciousness and possess a beautiful golden aura.

Ms. Jackson is the co-creator of Mystic Journeys, a Spiritual Retreats company that takes Lightworkers to portals, power chakra spots, and sacred places around the world. Her husband, Mystic D. Francis, co-facilitates these spiritual journeys with her. https://mysticjourneys.us/

Jill lives in Mississippi with her beloved husband D. Francis and their five dogs.

www.ingramcontent.com/pod-product-compliance
Lightning Source LLC
Chambersburg PA
CBHW061653120626
46550CB00003B/928